PLAZA

Wallpaper

IN DECORATION

PLAZA

Wallpaper
IN DECORATION

Jane Gordon Clark

WATSON-GUPTILL PUBLICATIONS / NEW YORK

WALLPAPER IN DECORATION

First published in the United States in 2001 by Watson-Guptill Publications,
a division of BPI Communications, Inc., 770 Broadway, New York, NY 10003
www.watsonguptill.com

Library of Congress Catalog Card Number: 00-110046

ISBN 0-8230-5623-6

First published in the United Kingdom in 2001 by Frances Lincoln Limited,
4 Torriano Mews, Torriano Avenue, London NW5 2RZ

This edition was designed and edited by Walton and Pringle for Frances Lincoln Limited
www.waltonandpringle.com

Picture research Caroline Thomas and Julia Pashley

Printed in Singapore

1 2 3 4 5 6 7 8 9 / 09 08 07 06 05 04 03 02 01

*To everyone who has worked for
Ornamenta, past and present, and
especially Catherine Fairweather,
Matilda Bathurst, Alexa Turnbull,
Melanie Taylor, Sally Crawford,
Marc Lefebvre and Louise Latham*

OPPOSITE *The simple floral sprig dotted
at intervals around the wall is a timeless
design style for wallpaper whose
popularity never fades whatever
current fashion dictates.*

contents

introduction

After years of being the 'Sleeping Beauty' of good decorating – always there in the background but never exciting decorators with any passion – wallpaper's merits are being reevalued. A few designers, recognizing wallpaper's true potential, are challenging its conservative image by experimenting with innovative techniques, using a combination of computer-aided skills and craftsmanship. But they have to try hard to get their designs noticed, for people have prejudices about wallpaper that blinds them to its virtues.

The common perception of many wallpapers is of huge quantities of relatively undistinguished mass-produced papers – repetitive in design, inconsequential in colouring and above all cheap – to be picked up in DIY stores. Yet, far from being a byword for mindless utilitarian patterned cover-up, wallpaper is fast becoming a positive force in decorating.

The virtues of good wallpaper lie in its variety and its ability to conjure up different moods in a room. It is unique in its potential for introducing an infinite choice of design, and brings a high degree of finish, clothing the walls with a richness and warmth, while at the same time creating an atmosphere. Walls are large spaces and the impact their decoration will have on a room can be more decisive in defining style than any other item – carpets, curtains, furniture or pictures. The combination of colour and pattern in a pleasing design will lift the spirit: a beautiful paper will give pleasure every time you enter a room.

Inspired by the past – when wallpapers were produced to replicate luxurious textiles and the decorative architectural details common to grand interior schemes – modern-day wallpaper designers are responding to the demands of a pared-down style of contemporary interior decoration by imitating hard surfaces, such as rough plaster and natural fabrics like raffia. Texture is a key element in contemporary interiors and wallpaper is no exception. Some of the most dynamic papers are those which not only use texture, but exploit the effects of a light-reflective flat surface. Many modern papers use metallic paints and powders to dazzling effect and are uncompromisingly graphic in design, yet blend into modern or more traditional schemes when printed in varying tones of the same colour.

The use of colour in wallpaper design has also evolved. Over the last few decades, many wallpapers had an aged, 'dipped in tea' look but now there is a new freshness in the available colour palette. Wallpapers are being printed in colours of wonderful clarity and some of the most beautiful papers also have a translucency which makes the colours literally glow with life. Even more dynamic are the colour results produced on paper by computer-aided technology and photographic reproduction. Although this technology is still expensive, the possibilities for colour for future designers is very exciting.

Ideas about the scale of the pattern in wallpaper design are also changing. There is a new confidence about using simple, largescale images which once might have seemed too imposing. In fact, largescale designs look terrific, even in small rooms. A classic designer's trick is to overscale some items in a room to add drama, and it works with wallpaper too.

In recent years, decorating a room with emulsion paint has been by far the most popular choice, perhaps because it is seen as a relatively undemanding and inexpensive decorating option. In my experience, people seem to worry that they do not know enough about wallpaper and lack confidence in their ability to achieve

ABOVE *Panels from a series of Chinoiserie wallpapers are designed to hang in sequence around the room. Hand-painted by artists in China today, they accurately reproduce the themes and techniques of eighteenth-century Chinese wallpapers.*

OPPOSITE *This contemporary design is based on a matrix of squares. The pattern is created by hand-screen-printing. Every area has a different strength of light-reflecting metallic ink.*

successful results. Common questions include: How do I calculate how many rolls of paper to buy? Will a small design get lost in a big room? Will a large design look too big in a small space? What will the design look like repeated over a large area? This book addresses those issues, and shows how wallpaper has the advantage over paint in that you can see exactly what the result will be even before the paper goes up on the wall. Wallpaper looks professional and polished, and gives a high degree of finish to the decoration. Above all, it enables you to define the character of any room. It allows you to make an individual statement about your own style and the way you like to live.

Wallpaper printing

Some of the milestones in papermaking and printing have had a telling effect on wallpaper's appearance and impact; others have simply streamlined aspects of the production process. But while up-to-date techniques may explore new effects made possible by technological discoveries, some manufacturers still take pains to imitate the mellower appearance of classic printing techniques. Indeed, some

OPPOSITE *A classic stripe given a contemporary makeover by printing extra-wide bands of two-toned stripes and punctuating them with silver lines. The luminosity and richness of the colour are a result of skilled hand-printing.*

BELOW *A neo-classical mural panel has been reproduced photographically from an early nineteenth-century wallpaper design. The original (see page 23) was hand-blocked using hundreds of separate woodblocks to build up the picture. Photographic reproduction gives the same effect for a fraction of the cost.*

RIGHT *Digital wallpaper technology gives the artist the freedom to create images in a kaleidoscope of colours and on a scale which can fill an entire wall with a single design. This design was created as an installation for an art exhibition, but could be equally striking in a domestic setting, hung as a frieze or a panel.*

of today's finest and most expensive papers are still actually hand-printed – often from original blocks – or are new designs printed by traditional methods.

The earliest Western wallpapers were all block-printed, and the process has continued to be used since the sixteenth century. Archive hand-blocked papers today are easily recognized by their rich, chalky colour, which forms into a vague outline around the printed area when the block is lifted. Slight irregularities in the register of different colours add to the charm and appeal of handmade designs, an effect which is often copied by machine-printed papers.

The hand-blocking process today is much as it was in the past. Designs are cut on blocks of seasoned hardwood and printed one colour at a time. Each colour requires a different block, and some papers need large numbers of blocks to complete their design. Fortunately, the original blocks used for some of the older designs are still available, which makes reprinting them today economically viable. Creating new blocks for these already costly papers can be very expensive.

In block-printing, the paper is fed in a continuous roll over a padded table. The block is dipped in a tray of colour and moved across to the printing table to be lowered and pressed with a lever onto the paper's surface. The whole run of paper is printed with the first colour and dried before the next can be started: a tiny pin at the corner of the block makes a register mark so that subsequent colours are printed in the right place.

In the nineteenth century, block-printing methods were superseded by machine-printing, and many designs adapted easily to the new techniques. This mechanical production process brought with it the advantage of a lower price, expanding the market for wallpaper and making it possible for every household to afford papers to decorate their walls. By the 1840s patterns were being transferred to the paper by means of an engraved copper cylinder or rollers with a design raised on the surface. The technique of printing designs in several colours quickly followed.

In many Victorian wallpapers, pride in technical skill and the possibility of using up to eight colours soon outstripped design merit. In part, the Arts and Crafts movement, led by William Morris and other artists and craftsmen who wanted to make beautiful things available to the new mass market (see page 28), was a reaction to such design excesses as these gaudy, machine-printed papers.

The Arts and Crafts design renaissance also breathed new life into the art of block-printing, and some of the blocks made by companies like Morris & Co and John Perry still exist and are in use.

The Arthur Silver studio, established in 1880, produced thousands of designs for wallpapers and textiles. Silver, and designers such as William Shand Kydd, utilized hand-stencilling techniques to transfer their patterns to a variety of paper types. Today, although hand-blocking and hand-stencilling are both still used to create hand-printed wallpapers, hand-screen-printing is more common. Screen-printing, like block-printing, is a time-consuming process: the colours are laid on one at a time, and a separate screen is needed for each colour. The main benefit of screen-printing is the opportunity large screens offer the designer to work on a grand scale.

The spirit of the past is still prevalent in wallpaper as many of the designs in current production were created decades or even centuries ago. The historical evolution of wallpaper patterns is explored throughout this book as it helps us to understand the origins of many popular wallpaper motifs.

ABOVE *Wallpaper which breaks down the barrier between art and craft is made in the manner of a David Hockney photo-montage. The clothing and other possessions of the room's owner have been photographed, greatly enlarged, and pasted to the walls in order to build up a unique three-dimensional collage.*

Wallpaper as art

More recently individual designers and specialist wallpaper companies have been moving away from the repeat pattern common in wallpaper design. No longer content to look back to the rich archive of patterns from the past, designers and artists are creating wallpaper which clearly reflects our own time. Photographic images and digital techniques – as well as a fresh approach to block- and screen-printing – have made it possible to design papers that can cover an entire wall with no visible repeat. The result has been the closing of the gap between art and what we think of as wallpaper – a shift that has interesting precedents in the work of twentieth-century artists and architects who experimented with wallpaper design (see pages 14-39).

Artists working on site-specific commissions have also been inspired to create wallpapers as a solution, sometimes painstakingly making each roll of wallpaper to achieve unique results. This exploration of wallpaper as an art form has, in turn, acted as a source of inspiration for large wallpaper manufacturers. Just as designer fashion inspires retailers, so gradually these new ideas in wallpaper design are beginning to filter down into the stores, making wallpaper designs which were originally rare and expensive available to all.

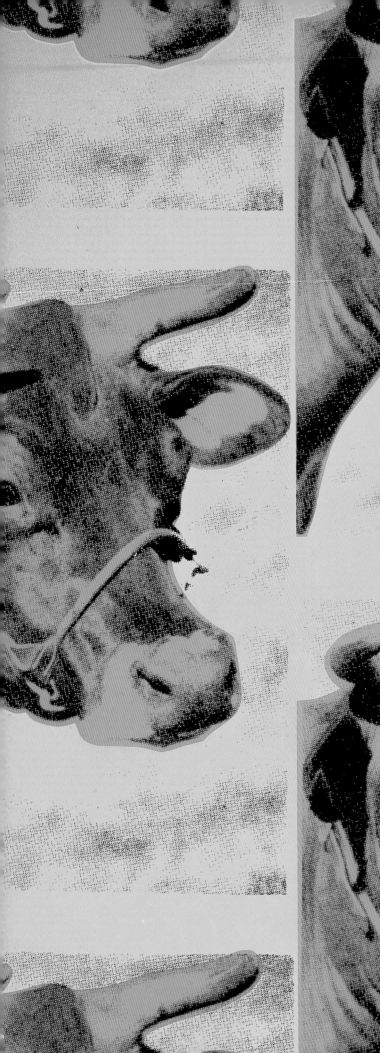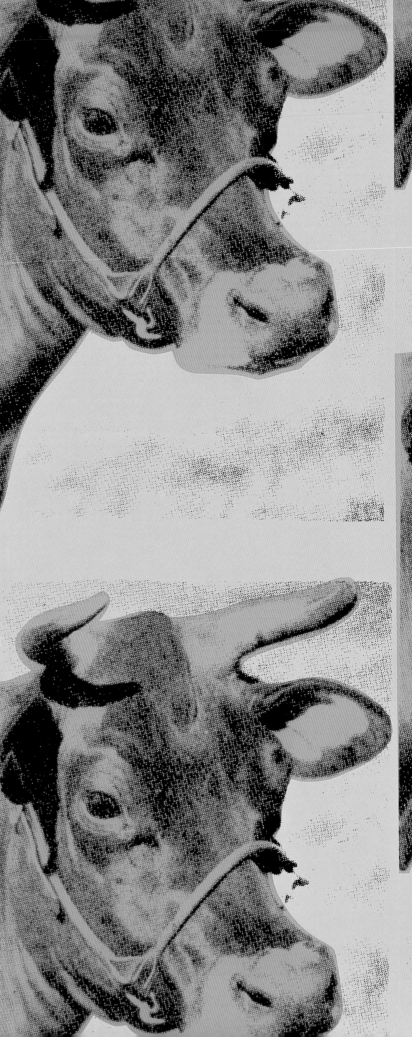

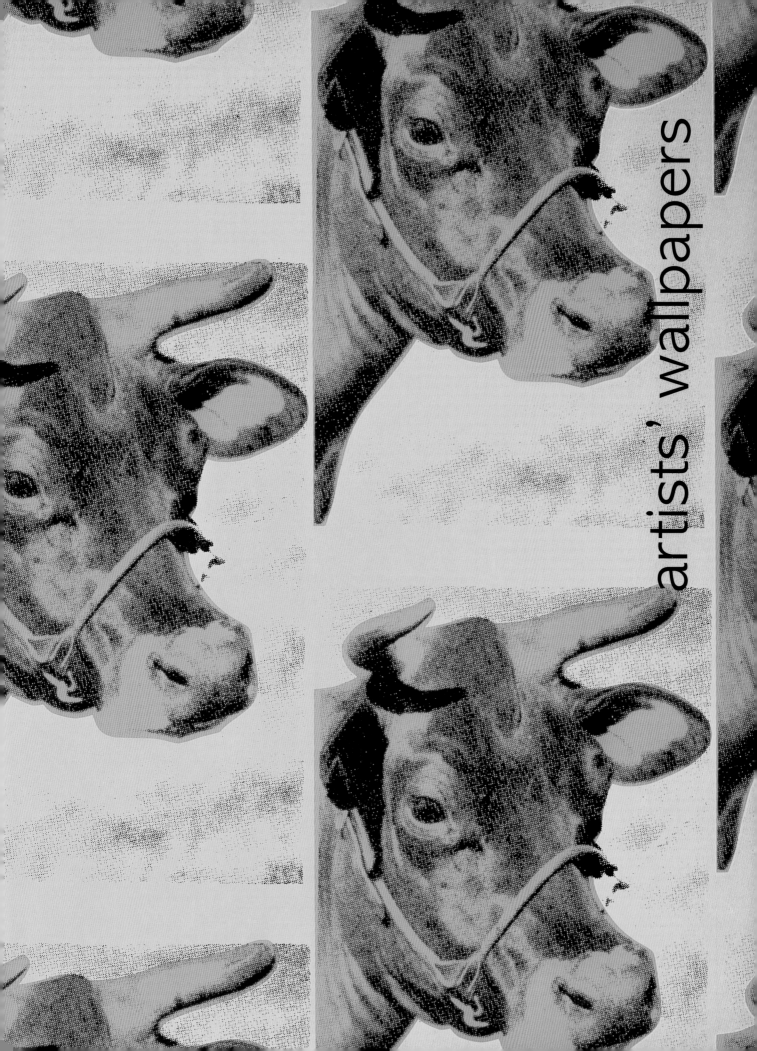

artists' wallpapers

designing wallpapers
Many great artists, illustrators and architects of the nineteenth and twentieth centuries – including William Morris, Frank Lloyd Wright, Andy Warhol, and Bridget Riley – have attempted to bridge the gap between the fine and decorative arts, which has led rather surprisingly to the production of stunning wallpaper designs. Many of these patterns on paper develop themes from the artists' work, while some artists have used wallpaper design as an opportunity to move in a different direction.

The demands of designing wallpaper are different from those of painting. Unlike the artist, the wallpaper designer is not asking the audience to stand and focus their attention on the composition in the same way that they are expected to view a painting. Wallpaper is not intended to undergo close scrutiny but because it covers a large expanse of wall, it is seen as one element in the decoration of the room.

The twentieth century saw many artists designing papers and enjoying pattern-making for its own sake, breaking away from the constraints of their chosen discipline. Alexander Calder, René Magritte, Marie Laurencin, Graham Sutherland and Andy Warhol created wallpaper, although many would say that Warhol's paintings of repeated images, such as Coca-Cola bottles or Campbell's soup tins, make the distinction between his wallpaper and art hard to define.

Architects were producing wallpapers too, perhaps viewing their designs as an extension of their role in shaping the interior space. The style and motifs used in papers designed by architects reflect their buildings, as can be seen in the wallpapers of A.W.N. Pugin, Charles Rennie Mackintosh, Frank Lloyd Wright and Le Corbusier, who all produced wallpaper designs complementary to their architectural style.

Some artists and architects have created wallpaper for specific places or to decorate their own rooms, perhaps as a result of a special commission, or simply in the interests of broadening the horizons of their work, but more usually, artists creating wallpaper work in the same way as any designer, making patterns for rooms that they will never see.

The beginnings of wall decoration

It is possible to trace the pedigree of pictorial wall decoration back to the murals of Knossos, Pompeii, Herculaneum and ancient Rome, with antecedents in Egyptian tomb decoration and prehistoric cave paintings. But it was the church frescoes of medieval Italy which led to the great secular flowering of mural painting during the Renaissance, when this form of decorative art reached its peak. Artists skilled in the use of perspective depicted colourful, dramatic scenes with intense realism on the palace walls of their rich patrons.

Wallpaper as wall decoration followed shortly after the invention of printing during the Renaissance. The name of Albrecht Dürer (1471-1528) seems an unlikely one to be associated with wallpaper, yet this German artist created two superbly drawn woodcuts specifically to be used as a repeating printed pattern to decorate the wall. The black-and-white natural forms of birds, leaves and grapes intertwine among the figures to create a complex pattern, which links with its mirror image to create a continuous design. These repeated designs were perhaps a natural progression from Dürer's interest in engraving.

ABOVE *This sixteenth-century woodcut print designed by Dürer shows a satyr family amidst a decorative vine pattern. Designed to link side to side and repeat top to bottom, this image works as a decorative mural.*

OPPOSITE *A modern reprint of the spectacular 'Hindustan' panorama. Over one thousand different blocks and eighty-five different colours were used to print the original, with its twenty panels designed to hang in a sequence.*

Pierre-Antoine Mongin designed 'Hindustan' for the Zuber company in 1807. He used as reference the carefully observed watercolours and drawings of Thomas and William Daniell, who had recently travelled in India. Alongside the fairly accurate portrayals of palaces, tombs and temples, his work incorporates charming elements of fantasy.

PREVIOUS PAGE *Using screen-printing techniques to create his iconic 'Cows' wallpaper design, Andy Warhol was able to bring his art to a much wider audience.*

ABOVE *It is possible to hang these papers on a canvas as individual panels. Occasionally, antique Chinese wallpaper panels can be found in salesrooms and antique shops.*

OPPOSITE *Hand-painted Chinese wallpapers are still being made today by artists in China and Hong Kong, whose skills in painting flowers, foliage and butterflies characteristic of these papers have been passed on through generations.*

With such auspicious beginnings in the hand of a great artist, the distinction of wallpaper would surely be assured. However, it was not until a century later that other artists' wallpapers appeared in the form of exquisitely coloured panels, painted by Chinese artists and designed to hang like a mural around the room.

Working with manufacturers who had developed refined techniques for producing wallpaper, European artists soon followed suit, creating wallpapers depicting imaginary and romantic scenes of exotic lands. These were printed by hand, using hundreds of different wood blocks.

These same nineteenth-century block-printing techniques were used later by artists and designers in the twentieth century to create their distinctive wallpapers. For example, William Morris, the famous designer of the Arts and Crafts movement in England, produced papers using these traditional block-printing methods, as did A.W.N. Pugin for the Palace of Westminster in London (see page 27).

Chinese wallpapers

The Chinese were also producing very rare hand-painted wallpapers in the seventeenth century for the export market in a tradition that continues today. The Chinese artists responsible for painting these exquisite papers by hand are unknown but their skills are evident in the surviving antique papers seen in English country houses today. It is a tradition which continues and hand-painted papers are still being exported from China and hung in contemporary houses. Produced in sets, they are designed to make a continuous but non-repetitive display around the room, each panel linking with the next. The earliest designs feature birds and flowers with foliage, painted on a background of plain colour, often pale blue, grey, cream or light green. The design is light and free and the drawing is in outline filled with clear bright colours. Branches of bamboo and flowering shrubs intermingle, while peonies and roses flower amidst waving grass. Birds, butterflies and other insects, painted with extraordinary botanical accuracy, fly, strut and perch among the leaves. A trellis or fence may be added at the bottom of some papers, changing angles as it winds around the room and giving the design a base.

Papers introduced after about 1750 became more complicated. They are narrative in composition, showing large numbers of people engaged in trading or daily activities such as farming, hunting, or making porcelain. Tea production was a frequent theme and workers are shown busily planting, harvesting, drying, packing and selling the tea.

The export of papers to Europe

When traders first began to bring Chinese wallpaper back to Europe at the end of the seventeenth century, the idea of hanging paper on the walls was already established but the sheer quality and originality of the Chinese imports easily surpassed anything else available. Soon the owners of great houses in England were clamouring for a Chinese room, hung with Chinese wallpaper, as a suitable background to a collection of Chinese lacquer furniture, vases, and ornaments. Since the paper was expensive it was only hung in important rooms, usually a principal bedroom.

During the eighteenth century the fashion spread throughout Europe and to America as well, and rooms with beautiful original Chinese wallpaper that is still intact can be seen in stately homes in England and old Colonial houses in America, today. At Temple Newsam, near Leeds in West Yorkshire, the Chinese wallpaper was hung as late as the 1820s, when the fashion was beginning to wane. Lady Hertford had received the paper as a gift from her admirer, the Prince of Wales, some years before. Perhaps she was not given sufficient paper, or perhaps she favoured a more highly decorated room, but to cover up the blank spaces she carefully cut out extra birds from John James Audubon's recently published *The Birds of America* and pasted them up as required. Such a solution is hardly to be recommended with Audubon prints today, but it illustrates the way in which a certain amount of judicious cutting out and pasting was to be expected to ensure continuity and harmony in the arrangement of the panels, particularly in awkward places where architectural features break the expanse of wall. Indeed, both plain, undecorated rolls and pieces with extra painted birds or butterflies were often supplied with the main panels.

It is not difficult to see why Chinese wallpapers have always been so highly prized. Not only are they completely different from any other form of wallpaper, they are beautifully executed paintings which can completely transform a room.

It is possible to obtain historic Chinese papers today from certain specialist dealers – at prices that reflect their rarity. Considerably cheaper alternatives are contemporary imports of hand-painted Chinese papers executed in the traditional way or the faithful reproductions of original designs which are made by specialist studios in the West.

Many wallpapers are produced which replicate the effects of hand-painting. For more than two centuries, manufacturers have gone to great lengths to try to reproduce the impression of artists' brushstrokes by mechanical means. Modern manufacturing methods can produce impressions as light and translucent as watercolour, but more traditional printing methods rely on many different colours to build up a hand-painted look.

OPPOSITE *Chinese hand-painted panoramas are designed to form a continuous decoration around the room. In the eighteenth century some featured flowers and flowing branches decorated with exotic birds while others, such as this one, were more complex narrative compositions. They showed large numbers of people engrossed in daily activities, from weaving silk to growing tea, and provide fascinating insights into life in China at the time. Here people are shown arriving at a tea house for the social ceremony that was an important aspect of civilized Chinese life.*

LEFT *The passion for Chinese wallpaper was so widespread in the eighteenth century that many grand country houses in England had at least one room decorated in this way. This beautiful paper, with an unusual silvery white background, is in Burton Constable Hall near Hull, England.*

French Réveillon papers

Chinese wallpapers established a taste for beautiful hand-printed wallpapers and encouraged European artists, especially in France and England, to be more creative in their designs. One of the most famous was the French wallpaper maker Jean-Baptiste Réveillon, whose papers are still regarded as supreme examples of the art. For some years before the French Revolution his factory in Paris produced the finest and most beautiful wallpapers for the French aristocracy; when it was sacked by the angry mob in 1789, Réveillon fled to England. But the factory was reopened later by others who found favour with the Revolutionaries – by designing patriotic papers in red, white and blue – and so were often allowed to continue the production of these earlier, more elegant designs.

Some of the most exquisite of Réveillon's papers took their inspiration directly from the painted decoration used by Renaissance artists to embellish wooden panelling, walls, doors and shutters. Raphael, for example, decorated the rooms of the Vatican palace in Rome with ancient Roman motifs, and soon afterwards his designs were copied in palaces all over Europe. Réveillon successfully adapted the effect for wallpaper. Classically inspired, the papers feature long vertical designs of urns, flowers, curve-necked swans, birds and beasts in graceful arabesques, block-printed in dozens of colours. The designs flow from a central stem which evolves upwards, interrupted by plaques and roundels containing figure compositions. They were usually intended to be hung as panels, separated by borders and plain wallpaper sections.

Réveillon's artists also took much of their classical inspiration from the archaeological excavations of the mid-eighteenth century, when the discovery of the Roman wall paintings of Pompeii and Herculaneum had considerable impact on contemporary taste. Undisturbed since Vesuvius erupted in AD 79, the decorations – which mostly consisted of large panels with ornate borders – were

OPPOSITE *The spectacular Réveillon wallpaper decorating the hallway of the Phelps-Hatheway House in Connecticut was imported from France in 1794. It incorporates favourite neo-classical devices inspired by the Roman wall-paintings excavated at Herculaneum and Pompeii. Such rich colouring and intricate designs surprise people accustomed to the blander tones and repetitive style of many modern wallpapers.*

BELOW *Réveillon's wallpapers have inspired many modern interpretations. The classical design (below left) was carefully copied from a paper hanging in the Phelps-Hatheway House. The paper next to it is also available today and is an interpretation of a design held in the manufacturer's archive.*

ABOVE *Many contemporary wallpapers such as this are inspired by the designs produced at the Réveillon factory in eighteenth-century Paris, but the true origins of these swirling arabesques and garlands of flowers flowing from a central stem are ancient Roman wall decorations.*

wonderfully preserved. Strongly contrasting Mediterranean colours – glowing reds, ochres, terracottas, rich greens, azure blues – were used together with large areas of black. Classical motifs, medallions and dancing figures filled the panel area with garlands, ribbons and flowers arranged symmetrically in graceful arabesques around a central motif. All were adapted and imitated in the new classical-style wallpapers produced by Réveillon (see pages 20-21). Many of the painters working for Réveillon had been trained in the Gobelins factory, creating designs for tapestries which share the same delicate elegance of style.

Their superb quality and artistry ensured Réveillon papers an appreciative market way beyond the shores of his native France. They were a very popular import in America during the eighteenth century and many can still be seen in New England houses.

Exact reproductions of Réveillon designs have been made by artists working for several eminent wallpaper manufacturers and, even more widely available, are freely adapted interpretations of the Réveillon style. These are produced to run as continuous wall-to-wall decoration rather than in panels, and with imagination they can be incorporated into many traditional interior design schemes.

Panoramic scenes

The Chinese concept of a continuous pictorial decoration covering all the walls of a room gave rise to European imitations. At the beginning of the nineteenth century a Western successor to the Chinese panorama emerged (see page 24), from European manufacturers who were now capable of printing wallpaper of high quality and considerable sophistication. As an astonishing decorative and technical achievement, the panoramic papers developed by the Zuber company of Rixheim, France and by Dufour in Mâcon and Paris have never been equalled.

A panoramic paper is like a continuous mural painting, but instead of being commissioned specially and painted *in situ* over months or years by an individual artist, these landscapes were designed by artists to be block-printed by hand onto rolls of wallpaper. Never before had wallpaper printing been attempted on such a scale. In order to cover the walls of large rooms without repeating a scene, twenty or thirty lengths were printed; some panoramic sets required up to fifty. Each length was about 3m (10ft) high by 50cm (20in) wide. Printing them called for thousands of hand-carved blocks and hundreds of colours. Creating even one

ABOVE *Scenic wallpapers designed in neo-classical style to look like hand-painted murals by artists Louis Lafitte (1770-1828) and Méry-Joseph Blondel (1781-1853). This is one of a series taken from the myth of Cupid and Psyche. It was printed by the French wallpaper manufacturer Dufour in grisaille (shaded tones of grey) using hundreds of woodblocks.*

panorama meant an enormous investment of time and risk for the manufacturers in what was then a completely new concept in interior decoration. And yet their entrepreneurial daring paid off. The panoramas were an immediate success and found an enthusiastic market in Europe and the United States throughout the nineteenth century, though they were never popular in England.

The popularity of the papers lay not in the technical skill behind them, but in their unique ability to break through space. The viewer is no longer conscious of being confined within the walls of a room, but by a trick of the eye is apparently outdoors, surveying an infinitely distant horizon. The artists took care to alternate close-up detail, scenes in the middle distance and glimpses of the horizon to achieve their effects. Zuber artists were especially skilled at creating an illusion of ever-deepening space by their realistic printing of the sky. They had perfected a technique to produce an even gradation of tones from the palest yellow or pink tinge on the horizon to a deeper blue at the top of the panel. This was done before the woodblocks were used.

Scenic themes were also popular because they transported viewers to exotic locations far away from everyday life. The city-dweller could find escape in faraway lands, both real and imagined: he could surround himself with picturesque Alpine scenery or share the discoveries of Captain Cook in the South Pacific. Trade between France and North America flourished and scenic papers from the period can still be seen in Colonial houses in the United States; New

BELOW *French panoramic wallpapers introduced in the United States in the nineteenth century were received enthusiastically. They quickly became fashionable status symbols and enhanced the homes of many prosperous families, where they can often still be seen today. This scenic panorama draws the viewer into a landscaped garden in France.*

Such papers were never very popular in England – perhaps because the English were less attracted by this kind of visual trickery, perhaps because panoramas left little space to display the ancestral portraits with which they liked to surround themselves.

Englanders were intrigued with topographical views of distant Europe or proudly surrounded themselves with the spectacular "Views of North America" produced in 1834. In 1852 Zuber took advantage of a wave of nationalist feeling in the American market and republished this paper as "The War of American Independence", substituting the foreground figures so that Boston Harbor became the scene of the Boston Tea Party and once-peaceful landscapes turned into battle sites full of soldiers and smoke. Precise authenticity was not demanded in scenic wallpapers.

Classical mythology provided another rich source of subjects, and these panoramas were often printed in grisaille, imitating reliefs in various shades of grey, a technique perfected by Dufour (see page 23). These gradations of colour naturally required far fewer blocks to achieve their sculptural effect than did full-colour panoramas, but their understated quality has its own particular beauty.

Zuber, the same company that produced the great scenic panoramas of the nineteenth century, is today recreating some of them for modern use. Other companies produce designs based on similar themes, also printed by hand, but a taste for panoramic decoration is still expensive to indulge.

Panoramic artists

The names of the artists who painted these scenes from which the wallpaper panels were adapted are no longer familiar to us today, perhaps because their chosen medium was wallpaper and they worked on commissioned subjects especially for the manufacturers, but there is no doubting their artistry. Louis Lafitte (1770-1828) and Méry-Joseph Blondel, who were both winners of the distinguished *Prix de Rome*, worked together in creating the twenty-six panels which make up a series of panoramas depicting the saga of Cupid and Psyche (see page 23). The panels are in grisaille and the graduated tones of grey required immense subtlety of execution to create the depth and variation in the printed panels. The artists had to work in blocks of solid colour to take into account the printing technique and the manner of carving the design directly on to the wooden blocks.

ABOVE *So that potential purchasers could envisage the final effect, samples showed complete panoramas on a much-reduced scale. It was not necessary to order the whole run, and careful planning was needed to decide on the number of drops required and the best way to arrange them. These samples show 'Views of North America' at the top and below it, 'Hindustan', the modern reprint of which can be seen on page 15.*

ABOVE *A skilled craftsman block prints the 'Gothic Lily' pattern wallpaper designed by Pugin by hand.*

OPPOSITE *The 'Gothic Lily' pattern is one of several wallpapers designed in the 1840s by A.W.N. Pugin for the Palace of Westminster, London. Pugin, a distinguished Victorian architect and designer, was passionately interested in medieval style and among the leaders of the wave of interest in the Gothic Revival. Bold repeating patterns printed in vibrantly strong colours are the hallmark of his wallpapers. Here interlinking strapwork weaves around stylized Tudor roses and lilies on a background of rich forest green, which throws the design into prominence.*

This paper can still be printed today in any combination of colours, using the original wooden blocks.

A.W.N. Pugin's wallpaper commissions

The British artist and architect Augustus Welby Northmore Pugin (1812–1852) was chosen by his fellow architect Charles Barry to decorate the new Palace of Westminster, London. Block-printing was the method by which Pugin's wallpaper designs were realized because at that time there was no technique for making wallpaper other than hand-painting. Pugin's designs were printed onto the paper by master craftsmen. This in itself was a skilled job which required many years of apprenticeship to learn.

The block-printing technique was well-suited to repeat wallpaper designs, where the image appears again and again, because fewer wooden blocks were needed to create the design. Therefore the printing process was also completed at a faster rate than designs with a large, or no, repeat. The overall effect of Pugin's repeat papers is entirely different from the exotic panoramas made in France (see pages 23-25), where there was little or no repeat, and nearer to our contemporary view of wallpaper.

In his relatively short life, Pugin created dozens of different designs for this decorating commission, all based on a strongly formal Gothic style. His wallpaper designs incorporate medieval heraldic devices like the portcullis symbol of the Palace of Westminster, the coronet and intertwining strapwork, together with other symbols associated with England – the Tudor rose, the lion rampant, and the oak leaf. The interpretation is highly stylized and realized on a large scale which befits the grandeur of its setting. The colours are flat, rich, dense and vibrant and often in combinations which can look overpowering to the modern eye. But these are not papers to be hung in the average house where they would overwhelm a modest-sized room, even if they were to the taste of a passionate devotee of nineteenth-century Gothic.

The lofty and spacious dining room in the House of Lords, London, is hung with a Pugin design. The paper has an intense yellow background which is over-printed by a stylized red flower. The flower stands out from the bright background because of the intensity of colour which occurs when flock is used (see page 45).

Many of Pugin's designs use flock to achieve this effect, which is a complex process. To produce flock, millions of tiny shards of wool are shaken over the surface before the first printing of the design motif is dry. The paper is then shaken continually to ensure that the fibres adhere evenly to the surface. In France, in the early nineteenth century, this shaking process was performed by a line of young boys lying on their backs under the length of wallpaper, kicking furiously. The problem was that boys employed in flock wallpaper production developed a form of silicosis of the lungs, similar to that of young chimney sweeps. To spare the boys' health, the manufacturers began to use an alternative method of distributing the wool shards that involved a number of paddles.

Pugin's papers for the Palace of Westminster are a unique part of the British national heritage and as such are restored and maintained in beautiful condition. Whenever they become too worn or decayed they are replaced by facsimile reproductions, often printed from the same wooden blocks which were used in Pugin's time. Inevitably this is an expensive process and the resulting public hue and cry over wallpaper costing hundreds of pounds a roll usually resonates through the national newspapers. The Lord Chancellor's apartment in London is sometimes open to the public for visits so that these exquisite papers designed by Pugin can be seen *in situ*.

ABOVE *William Morris's 'Bower' wallpaper, first produced in 1877, demonstrates his superb handling of complex repeating patterns. Light and dark areas and large and small floral motifs are balanced in a lively overall decoration which intrigues the eye without resolving into any unintended shapes or distracting directional lines.*

OPPOSITE *In the Acanthus Room at Wightwick Manor, England built in the late 1880s and decorated in the Arts and Crafts taste, the original Morris wallpaper shows a confident use of large-scale design in a relatively small space. The twelve-block pattern of swirling leaves is taken past the picture rail to ceiling height. In the green-painted area behind the pictures the wallpaper was removed because of water damage.*

William Morris's patterns

The Arts and Crafts movement was formed by artists and painters who rejected what they saw as the lofty pretensions of their contemporaries concerning the value and purpose of pure art. They were happy to cross disciplines and were as satisfied working in the applied arts – producing designs for a wider public – as they were in creating fine art and architecture in its purest forms. It is an attitude which resonates back to the Renaissance era, but finds particular expression in the thinking of designers such as William Morris.

William Morris's wallpaper designs present a softer and slightly less formalized interpretation of the belief that pattern should be 'honest', incorporating no tricks designed to deceive the eye. In contrast to the rather static emblematic motifs of the Gothic-style patterns (see page 27), Morris's wallpapers have a strongly organic quality. He followed the design principle that forms should be abstracted from nature and stylized, not just a direct imitation of nature. His plants are recognizable and graceful; though painted in areas of flat colour, often with firm outlining, the flowers flow and curve across the paper. There is no modelling in darker and lighter tones, but a feeling of depth is created by shading in strong parallel lines. His leaves and stems intertwine as if blown by a light breeze, their natural forms flowing freely despite being rendered in only two dimensions. Above all, he used the idea of the repeat in a masterly way, demonstrating his ability 'to mask the construction of our pattern enough to prevent people from counting repeats'.

The influence of William Morris and his fellow members of the Arts and Crafts movement – and subsequent followers, such as C.F.A. Voysey – has been incalculable, changing people's ideas of decoration first in England and then in the United States. Morris's name is a household word, a status few designers have ever achieved. His patterns are still popular, not just for wallpapers and fabrics, but scaled down and adapted to all sorts of domestic items.

Making good design affordable

The concept underpinning Morris's designs – that of a two-dimensional flat pattern repeating as the block-printing process allows – worked superbly for him, but once exposed to a mechanized manufacturing process it has, in lesser hands, led to thousands of unimaginative and repetitious wallpapers. Morris wanted to make the best in craftsmanship and design available to a wider society. The manufacturing process itself has indeed enabled the price of printing wallpaper to tumble, making it a commodity affordable to everyone, but the quality of design in the cheapest papers is often depressingly dull. This may explain why reproductions of 'classic patterns', particularly small decorative motifs and floral designs, are so popular. This is not simply part of a fashion for the antique, but a recognition of the enduring quality of these traditional designs.

The artists who worked with William Morris, and many of those who immediately followed, were strongly influenced by his ideas and the artistic techniques he developed for their execution. Even more significantly, Morris's influence gave a new status to wallpaper design, and to the product itself, which gained popularity amongst artists and the wider public. Wallpaper had a far greater importance in people's homes, and artists, illustrators and architects of distinction were perfectly happy to design wallpapers.

The acceptance of wallpaper design as an art form and the desire of artists to practise a range of different arts and crafts is shown in the work of artist, illustrator and designer Walter Crane (1845-1915) and the architect C.F.A. Voysey (1857-1941), who both produced memorable wallpaper designs. Although today Walter Crane is probably best known for his children's book illustrations, at the end of the nineteenth century he was widely admired as a wallpaper artist, creating original and beautifully drawn papers strongly influenced by the current vogue for Art Nouveau. He also produced many designs for children's wallpapers, which evolved naturally from his book illustrations. His lovely design called 'Sleeping Beauty' shows the recumbent figure of Sleeping Beauty herself about to be woken by her prince, intertwined with a swirling arabesque arrangement of wild roses, leaves, and thorns. It displays the romanticism of the time and a magical narrative quality which would probably still enthral young girls today.

Voysey was a follower of Morris's ideas and the Arts and Crafts movement in general, but he developed a style which was uniquely his own. Voysey had a strangely English attitude to the influence of Art Nouveau, which he considered a distinctly unhealthy, foreign thing, and yet the influence of Art Nouveau can be seen in his wallpaper designs. Voysey produced wallpapers with flat areas of solid colour, making no attempt to give his work depth, instead creating the rhythm of pattern through balance and tone.

Voysey's reputation as an Arts and Crafts architect has far outlived his work as an artist and designer, yet he was a widely respected wallpaper artist during this time, producing over two hundred wallpaper designs in the course of a long and productive career, works which are distinguished by their originality and simple charm.

Voysey's wallpapers were admired by other architects, who used them in their own interior schemes, and his influence on the way other designers approached the demands of printed pattern and the restrictions of the repeated image can clearly be seen, not only in subsequent wallpapers but also in fabric design.

During this period an interest in wallpaper seems to have been an integral part of the architects' approach to interiors, and with both Pugin and Voysey it was a fairly logical development of their architectural ideas – Pugin with his passion for the medieval Gothic style, Voysey with his simpler Arts and Crafts style.

The Bloomsbury set

Despite the pared-down simplicity pioneered by Voysey, some artists were still producing highly decorative patterns. Down in the depths of rural Sussex, England, in a seventeenth-century farmhouse, the Bloomsbury set were embellishing their walls, and almost everything else besides. Here the artists Duncan Grant (1885-1978) and Vanessa Bell (1879-1961) lived intermittently with their artistic and literary friends who had decamped from the Bloomsbury district of London (hence their name). In between painting and making ceramics, Duncan Grant and Vanessa Bell lavished their attention on decorating their farmhouse. They painted decoration on every possible flat surface of their furniture – the beds, the chairs, the tables and cupboards were all covered in their characteristic designs and patterns, filled with languid figures, flowers, foliage, fish, shells, urns and other natural and organic forms which could enhance their presence. Their technique of freely flowing brushstrokes and chalky matt paint

OPPOSITE *A flat, stylized pattern of doves and leaves designed by Voysey for machine-printed wallpaper illustrates his passionate belief for simplicity in design.*

superbly conveys their unique spirit and imagination. On the walls in the dining room a truly original design has been stencilled as wallpaper. Not many people are brave enough to use black wallpaper, or even black paint, on their walls. But this wallpaper design has a black background, a decision which could only have been made by a painter who understands the use of colour and knows that black can resonate warmth and a sense of enclosure – quite apart from being a striking background for objects and people. On top of the black background the artists have stencilled a block design in a chalky white paint, and then drawn lines freehand in yellow paint between the squares. The effect mirrors the formal pattern of traditional wallpaper design but so freely applied it creates a painterly sense of abandon.

In the drawing room the same technique has been used by Vanessa Bell to paint a paisley pattern paper in soft shades of grey and white. It produces a gently restful atmosphere in the room, which is otherwise filled with a large number of eclectic objects and a striking painted mantelpiece.

Several of the fabrics which Duncan Grant designed for the house have been reproduced and, at some stage, have been available to a wider public, but sadly the wallpapers have never been reproduced. Perhaps manufacturers think that wallpapers designed by artists are too idiosyncratic for widespread public acceptance. Yet, having a paper designed by Vanessa Bell would be an original choice from amongst the general run of wallpaper on offer as to be positively life-enhancing and worth planning a decorating scheme around.

Architects' wallpaper designs

In contrast to the freehand approach to wallpaper design of Duncan Grant and Vanessa Bell is the measured technique adopted by Frank Lloyd Wright (1869-1959) and Le Corbusier (1887-1965). As architects and designers, their names are synonymous with a pared-down style – that stark simplicity which has led generations to choose plain white walls for their interior decoration, rather than anything more colourful or inclined to make a statement. In view of this, it is fascinating to discover that two of the twentieth century's defining architects were both interested in wallpaper decoration. Who would have imagined Le Corbusier, with his passion for purity and minimalism, would have chosen to embellish his walls with wallpaper, let alone create his own designs? But Le Corbusier was a painter as well as an architect, so perhaps it was a combination of these disciplines which led him to design wallpaper in patterns which were dramatic departures from wallpaper patterns that had gone before.

Abstract papers

Many of Le Corbusier's wallpapers use solid colours, and were designed to hang either by themselves or in any combination of colours the client wanted. Other papers conceived by the architect present bold graphic designs of solid colour blocks, arranged with the utmost simplicity to form a design on the wall and cleverly contrived to allow a variety of different combinations. The scale is grand. The colours are limited. The effects are stunning. Although they were originally conceived in the early twentieth century, the would not look out of place in a contemporary loft apartment at the beginning of the twenty-first century, if someone was brave enough to manufacture them again.

OPPOSITE *Wallpaper designed and made in situ by Duncan Grant and Vanessa Bell to decorate the dining room of their Sussex farmhouse. The square blocks were stamped over a black background and the chevron lines were added by hand.*

In comparison to those of Le Corbusier, Frank Lloyd Wright's wallpaper designs are more geometric and at the same time more complex. Every element looks as if it has been drawn with a ruler, as indeed it was, and measured out with extreme precision. Many of the shapes on his papers play tricks with the eye, making patterns move and dance and change form across the flat surface of the wall. The colour palette is bright and very carefully balanced to achieve the required effect – strong colours build upon lighter ones to make the complex rhythm of the design. These are papers which make a bold statement in their own right, and a Frank Lloyd Wright paper hung on one wall only could be all the decoration required in a room.

Contemporary with Frank Lloyd Wright was the sculptor Alexander Calder (1898-1976). His best-known works are his extraordinary mobiles, an art form in which he excelled. These strange, amoeba-like shapes hang suspended from one another, like a three-dimensional family tree, each piece moving independently – yet dependent on the main lines of suspension. One of his most intriguing pieces hangs in the Guggenheim Museum in New York.

Calder's diversity of artistic interest extended beyond three-dimensional works to two-dimensional designs for wallpapers and wall hangings. He was strongly influenced by the artist Joan Miró (1893-1983), whose spiky forms and bright primary colours find a resonance in Calder's wallpaper designs. They are conceived on a grand scale with giant splodges of colour which dramatically impose themselves upon the room, demanding furniture of the utmost simplicity.

Experiments with the repeated image

Andy Warhol (1927-1987) experimented frequently with the repeated image in his art, using the same disciplines and restrictions that the wallpaper artist has to contend with. In his multiple portrait of Marilyn Monroe, for example, her face is photographically replicated four times on the same canvas. The image remains the same, but the colouring of the face, the lips, the hair and the background change each time. Warhol was fascinated by this idea of the repeated image, partly for its own sake and partly because, like William Morris (see page 28), he wanted his art to be available to as many people as possible. The silk-screen technique suited his work: flat areas of solid colour and line drawing works just as well when screen-printed as it does in the original artwork. His pictures of endlessly repeated Coca-Cola cans are even more repetitive, because they are all identical. He makes a statement in this way about mass production and the mechanical process of manufacture. It is a comment on brash materialism and popular culture, made more apparent for being endlessly repeated.

It is not a big step, then, to the making of wallpaper. His famous 'Cows Wallpaper' (see pages 12-13) in which the image of a cow's head is repeated identically down the paper is the same in conception as the image of Marilyn Monroe. It is also screen-printed in the same way and makes the same slightly shocking impact on the viewer.

In 1966, Warhol announced that he wished to free himself from the restraints of making painting and sculpture. The result of this shift away from fine art was the production of 'Cows Wallpaper', which he exhibited at the Leo Castelli Gallery in New York, where he covered the rear room of the gallery in the paper. Warhol took the image of the cow from an agricultural journal which he found when browsing in a secondhand bookstore. His passion for repeating imagery reached

OPPOSITE *Hand-printed wallpaper designed by Frank Lloyd Wright and made by silk screen printing. The geometric design shows the balance of shape and colour the artist needs to achieve in order for the motif to form a rhythm on the wall which is comfortable to the eye.*

an extreme point here, as he chose to paper entire walls with the powerful image of this mechanically replicated cow's head.

British artist Graham Sutherland's (1903-1980) two wallpaper designs look so different from anything else he did that it would be impossible to identify him as the artist without more information. In 1950, just prior to the great explosion of British design talent heralded by the Festival of Britain, Graham Sutherland designed a wallpaper for the mass market based on the word 'OXO', that little square of brown meat stock which gets crumbled up to make gravy. It seems an odd inspiration, especially as the resulting wallpaper is more reminiscent of the curly undulations of seaweed than anything to do with cooking. Diners at the famous OXO tower restaurant, London are just as unlikely to be confronted with OXO cube gravy as they are to see the walls decorated with Graham Sutherland's eponymous wallpaper, which seems a missed opportunity really, given that he is one of the major British artists of the twentieth century.

Matisse's paper murals

Towards the end of his life, when he was too frail to paint, Henri Matisse turned to a new way of expressing his visual ideas. Brightly coloured papers took the place of his paints and a pair of scissors replaced his brushes. Together with a team of assistants he cut out freely flowing forms of natural vegetation, flowers and fig leaves, dancing figures and abstract shapes. He worked freehand and without any preliminary drawing, pasting the shapes to the walls to make huge paper murals. These vibrant images, full of movement and life, have become icons of contemporary art, often reproduced as posters and cards, their sharp-edged images imprinting themselves on the mind of the viewer and providing inspiration for later artists and designers.

But paper stuck to the wall is not necessarily wallpaper. For Matisse it was more a way of exploring his ideas in a different medium and thus being inspired by the materials to create something unique. They were one-off, site-specific installations, never intended for reproduction as wallpaper, though as images they have been reproduced so often as postcards and prints that they have become some of the most familiar images of the artist's oeuvre.

Bridget Riley's decorative papers

The challenge of creating a work of decorative art for a particular location was presented to the distinguished British artist Bridget Riley (b. 1931) in the 1980s. The unlikely combination of enlightened health officials at the Royal Liverpool Hospital, the Director of the Liverpool Art Gallery and a group of philanthropic Liverpudlians conceived the idea of commissioning contemporary artists to enliven the long corridors of what was then the largest hospital in Europe. Bridget Riley's response was excitingly architectural in conception and highly charged in decorative drama. She had recently returned from a trip to Egypt, where she had seen the tombs of the Pharoahs. The tombs greatly influenced her thinking about how to decorate the plain hospital space. Just as the ancient Egyptians 'faked' the architectural features in their tombs, painting in cornice, frieze and skirting (base) board, so Bridget Riley developed her idea for a wallpaper decoration. She was already presented with a rather narrow black skirting (base) board and a wide band of black rubber at dado height to stop hospital equipment from bumping the

OPPOSITE *This hand-block-printed abstract design was produced by Graham Sutherland for the wallpaper manufacturers Cole & Son in 1950. It was one of twelve papers in a folio of sample wallpapers for 'Wallpaper for a Small Home' issued by the Council of Industrial Design.*

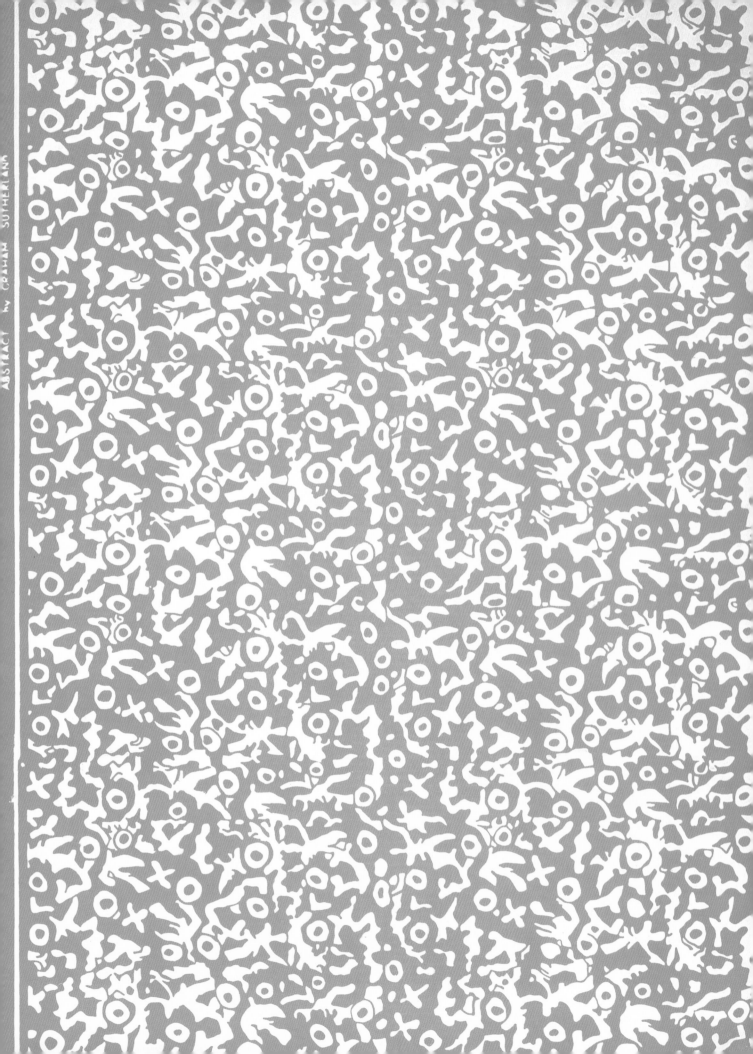

ABSTRACT by GRAHAM SUTHERLAND

Study for Royal Liverpool Hospital (Blue)
1981 Bridget Riley.

walls. So she added another black band higher up and made a cornice. Between these divisions she added bands of colour.

The ancient Egyptians lived for thousands of years with a fairly limited colour palette: turquoise, blue, red, yellow, green, black and white – colours with dense pigments which absorb and glow with the brilliant light of North Africa. Bridget Riley imposed upon herself similar restrictions in colour range and chose to print in solid bands of black, white, blue, ochre and pink. The bands of colour run down the corridor and turn a sharp right angle at the end to arrest the eye, before opening into a wide archway. The effect is a dazzling expression of the artist's work and cannot help but brighten the spirits of those who live and work in the somewhat austere world of a hospital.

Contemporary artists' papers

The idea of printing patterns on walls as a form of artistic expression is gaining currency among today's young artists. Individuals are experimenting with new techniques made possible by computer-driven technology to create images that are far larger than is possible using traditional printing methods (see page 109). Some ambitious young artists are even creating site-specific installations using the repeated image to create works of art, while others are turning their paintings into wallpaper using screen-printing methods (see page 112) to recreate the image on a continuous roll of paper, once again blurring the division between art and decoration.

In the nineteenth and twentieth centuries, artists, architects, scupltors and illustrators were responsive to the idea of working in the applied arts, but more recently there has existed a barrier between the disciplines which fine artists have rarely crossed. In 1982 Bridget Riley was unusual in her enthusiastic response to a wallpaper commission and there are signs now that others are following her lead. Contemporary galleries sometimes show artists' wallpapers as items worthy of exhibition, and in 1999 the Victoria and Albert Museum in London showcased several artists' wallpapers. More recently, an installation in a contemporary London gallery by a young British artist involved a room decorated in printed paper. At first glance the design covering the walls appeared to be simply a pattern of two adjacent ovals. Key to understanding this design, however, was a chair in the middle of the room. The chair seat was a pad of ink and the artist had created the paper by sitting naked in the ink and then sitting on the paper to create the design. But this is a 'one-off' installation, hardly suitable for any manufacturing process. More influential are the artists who recreate their paintings as wallpapers or who, like Andy Warhol (see pages 12-13), often see little difference between the two. When artists are interested in the impact of the repeated image, then wallpaper gives their art wider access.

Today young artists seem to have a more open and positive approach to the reproduction of their work, as prints, as postcards, and on occasions as very large-scale reproductions which can easily be described as wallpaper. A common view held by many artists is that they want their art to have a wider public beyond the few rich patrons who can afford to own the original, and printing large runs on panels of paper, rather than strictly limited editions, is a positive way that this can be achieved. Whether these large prints are seen as panels of wallpaper or repeated works of art becomes more a question of perception than of actual substance.

OPPOSITE *The design for Bridget Riley's Liverpool Hospital decoration was not practical to paint onto the walls, as the hallway for which it was intended was always immensely busy with human traffic. The design was screen-printed in panels onto vinyl and hung like a wallpaper.*

wallpaper designs

trompe l'oeil effects
Since its earliest beginnings in Europe, wallpaper has been produced in imitation of other, more expensive, wall finishes and furnishings. The chameleon capacity of paper to disguise itself is an endless source of delight. Paper can physically assume a third dimension by being coated with textured finishes or by various processes of embossing. But flat paper can also take on a convincing illusionist character by using patterns that deceive the eye with their three-dimensional simulation of light and shadow.

The range of dramatic, beautiful and witty effects created by the papermaker's art in the past continues to offer inspiration and the chance to be enterprising and original in decorating homes today. Totally different in concept from the stylized designs and cool abstraction of the flat repeating patterns, these papers bring the excitement of the unexpected and a flash of wit to the decoration.

Wallhangings of tapestry

The pictorial tapestries and stamped leather hangings that rank among the antecedents of wallpapers once decorated homes very different from those most of us live in today. But from the beginning, these materials inspired wallpaper makers, and it is interesting to trace some of the ways in which this inspiration has been reinterpreted over the years.

Tapestries have always been among the rarest and most expensive furnishings, and wallpapers have been inspired both by their imagery and by their texture. The rich verdure colours and woven effects of the old tapestries used as wallhangings have been wonderfully recreated in fine wallpaper. Papers with embossed stitched effects have something of the properties of fabric in softening an interior. The cocoon-like atmosphere evoked by their woven textures could be very appropriate in a winter room, warmed by a roaring log fire, for instance, or on the walls of a study or dining room. There is inspiration also in the way in which tapestry papers became popular for hallways and dining rooms in some homes at the turn of this century, where they harmonized with the fashion for neo-Jacobean furniture and stained oak woodwork.

Stamped leather

The effects possible from various simulations of stamped leather tend to be more grandiose, less domestic, in atmosphere. Long before the invention of wallpaper, embossed and gilded leather was highly prized for wallhangings as well as for various forms of upholstery. The techniques had been brought by Arabs from Morocco to Cordoba in Spain, and by the late seventeenth century fine workmanship was being produced by craftsmen in England, France and the Low Countries. It was natural for the earliest wallpapers to imitate the look and finish of contemporary leather and to draw on many of the same designs, from baroque ornamentation to motifs inspired by the new craze for *Chinoiserie*. Gilders easily turned their skills to making the new 'stampt' or 'imbost' papers, and some of their methods remained in use for years. A taste for authentic leather hangings persisted in parts of Europe through the eighteenth century, so an inexpensive alternative was provided by these high-quality wallpapers simulating leather, with

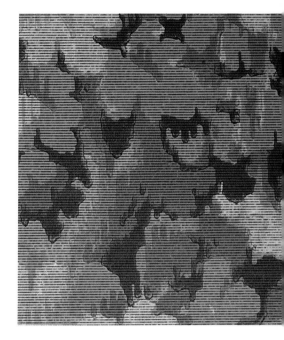

ABOVE *'Fontainebleau' wallpaper reprinted by Zuber from a nineteenth-century design achieves a remarkably realistic imitation of the thickly woven texture of tapestry.*

OPPOSITE *This lustrous paper imitates the look of fine silk, with a watered effect which is horizontal, rather than vertical. It is a classic wallpaper design cleverly reinterpreted for contemporary interiors.*

PREVIOUS PAGE *A cracked surface texture that resembles scorched plaster brings textural interest to a simple setting.*

embossed motifs decorated with metal foil and lustrous effects achieved with powdered silicates such as mica and talc.

There was a resurgence of taste for leather-like finishes at the turn of the eighteenth century. Beginning in the 1860s, Japanese 'leather paper' was imported into England and America and found its way into some grander houses. Although this paper was made by craftsmen in Japan, many of the highly embossed patterns were Western in style, recalling the exuberance of Renaissance and Baroque ornamentation on earlier wallpapers. As the fashion for things Japanese grew, some more motifs inspired by the Orient appeared.

In the late 1870s Lincrusta-Walton, a new material based on solidified linseed oil, was patented. Lincrusta was capable of imitating relief plasterwork and carving as well as stamped leather, and was the first of many products of similar composition which are usually classed as wallpapers. It was sold coloured, often

RIGHT *A new paper whose bumpy texture simulates the effect of crocodile skin. It is an up-to-date version of the kind of wallpapers made at the beginning of wallpaper manufacture, when papers were printed in imitation of fine Spanish leathers.*

with gilt ornamentation in typical leather fashion, or plain, to be painted or varnished *in situ*. The designs showed a typically Victorian gamut of influence: Celtic, Egyptian, Byzantine, and Oriental. Lincrusta and its imitators were widely used for dados, where they sometimes survive. When we see Lincrusta wallcoverings in old houses they usually look rather dull and brown, but this is often because the patina of the gilding has been lost, for they certainly started life as rich and lustrous as their seventeenth-century predecessors.

Luxurious textiles

One of the earliest and most enduring achievements of papermaking has been to imitate the textured effects of some of the most sumptuous fabrics. Materials such as cut velvet, with its relief figuring of downy pile; moiré silk, with its natural rippling watermark creating a waving pattern; and damask-woven silks, where a variation in the direction of the weave reflects light in areas of patterning, were all originally textile masterpieces produced by Italian weavers of the Renaissance which only the richest households could afford. Ingenuity was applied to create less costly textile imitations for use as wall hangings. Indeed, when flock papers began to be produced in the seventeenth century, the craftsmen simply applied the established process for making mock velvet to paper instead of cloth.

Flock paper is made by printing or stencilling a design in an adhesive onto paper and then lightly brushing minute wool or silk shavings over it. The fibres stick to the pattern and the background is left clear. The resulting contrast between the slightly raised surface of the textured flocking and the smooth ground looks very much like richly figured velvet. Some original examples are so realistic that when they are hanging on a wall, it is often actually hard to distinguish wallpaper from fabric.

Flock papers have a long and grand pedigree, and it is sad that the image of flock has been tarnished for many of us by the uninspiring sight of cheap modern versions adorning the walls of old-fashioned bars and restaurants. Museum conservationists and the curators of grand historic houses regard fine flock papers with suitable deference and respect, and skilfully produced examples are among the most richly textured wallpapers to be found. Flock papers produced in London were highly esteemed and were exported to Europe and North America in the eighteenth century. Mme de Pompadour chose a blue flock to line her closet at Versailles and, naturally, once the mistress of Louis XV had chosen it the fashion spread; walls and closets similarly papered were soon *de rigueur* in fashionable French society. Since flock papers were valued and cared for, some have actually survived in the great houses to which they lent an aura of magnificence. Others are copied and replaced when period interiors are restored.

If you want to hang good-quality flock paper, you can still buy hand-printed reproductions of the original designs. Flock papers can look appropriate and attractive in any period environment in rooms of sufficient grandeur to accommodate them. This does not necessarily imply great size: many designers have successfully incorporated rich flock papers into quite small rooms, where they introduce a background of great luxury and work as an interesting background for either contemporary or antique furniture, pictures and fabrics.

In textiles, damask patterns are created by varying the direction of threads in a single-colour weave; in paper the contrasting pattern areas can be imitated by printing matt-finish motifs onto a smooth, polished ground. Where the colour tone is identical or very similar, the effect closely resembles the fabrics that inspired

ABOVE *The rich texture of flock makes it particularly suitable for a period setting. This room at Rousham Park in Oxfordshire is hung on the upper part of the walls, above the panelled dado. A light coloured background contrasts with the deep red areas of patterning and enriches the effect of the flock.*

these wallpapers. This plays tricks with the eye: sometimes you see the background shapes as dominant, sometimes the pattern catches the eye. Often, however, two distinct or contrasting colours are used, which throws the pattern more clearly into relief. Although the elaborate designs often echo those of flock papers, the smooth surface of damasks makes the overall effect somewhat lighter.

Walls hung with real damask or flock were beyond the means of the seventeenth-century English diarist Samuel Pepys, who records that his wife's closet was done up in 'counterfeit damask'. Pepys would have wanted to emulate the rich hangings he admired in ceremonial state apartments which he encountered as Chief Secretary to the Navy. The new damask-effect paper was an affordable substitute which appealed to the rising professional class.

Traditional damask patterns are often not only intricate in outline but large in

RIGHT *A scaled down version of a damask design wallpaper contrasts with an almost plain companion paper.*

OPPOSITE *Renaissance damasks and brocade have always been a source of inspiration for wallpaper designers. The impact of the stylized foliage depends not just on scale but on the degree of tone and colour contrast between figure and ground. Some papers are designed to run fluently in continuous all-over patterns; others are based on motifs with a more static, majestic quality.*

scale. It is normal to see such papers decorating large spaces such as the drawing rooms of great country houses or hotel ballrooms. But scale alone should not preclude using revivals of these papers in more modern surroundings; recoloured versions of traditional designs could easily work in a contemporary setting. The designs are well balanced, with a harmonious relationship of pattern to background, and the very satisfactory evenness of this effect can keep large-scale damask designs from overwhelming a small room. Try hanging a single roll of a design you like in a corner of the room: you may be surprised how a pattern which looked intimidating in the sample book suddenly comes to life on the wall, fitting in with its scale and dimensions.

Moiré papers exploit the same principle of subtly contrasting matt and shiny areas of patterning, in this case in imitation of the magical effects created by the play of light on the natural iridescence of silk that has been watermarked, that is, treated by intense pressure, heat and water, or steam. Moiré papers contribute a beautifully quiet background, but with far more life than a flat painted wall. Traditional moiré texturing sometimes provided the ground for a printed motif and sometimes ran in ribbon-like bands between other stripe effects.

Wallpaper manufacturers now make a wide range of styles of moiré, ranging from small unobtrusive patterns where, from a distance, all you notice is a slight movement of colour, to much bolder designs where the contrast of light and shade is more positively marked (see page 42). Like large-scale damask designs, these grander moiré patterns are very difficult to judge close up. The pattern may seem random and abstract as a small sample, but once on a wall its rhythm is revealed and the magnificent silken effect achieved.

Floral and figurative papers

The fine printed patterns of fabric makers have always been a source of inspiration for wallpaper manufacturers. The two industries have often had much in common, although calico printers developed efficient machine-printing some half-century before wallpaper makers succeeded in mechanizing their process. Sometimes an attractive fabric print was taken and adapted for wallpaper, but just as important was the cross-fertilization of ideas from one medium to another.

An early influence on wallpaper designs came from the bright colours and exotic patterns of the chintzes imported by the trading companies from India. British and French imitations were soon produced in wallpapers as well as fabrics. By the end of the eighteenth century an increasing amount of European wallpaper featured the floral and figurative designs that have remained part of the tradition ever since. Manufacturers, particularly in France, had developed the skills and artistry to create fresh, lively motifs. The freer style owed a good deal to the influence of Oriental designs, and to the use of large woodblocks which allowed largescale repeats and overall continuity.

Flowers are always popular motifs for wallpapers, just as they are on fabrics, but whereas the folds of fabric partially obscure the design, wallpaper boldly reveals it, because it covers a large area and the design repeats over a flat expanse. This repetition on paper causes different patterns to emerge as the motif is repeated in diagonal or horizontal lines across the wall. Likewise tiny flower motifs can almost disappear looking like dots on the wall, while large-scale flowering branches, based on Indian 'Tree of Life' designs, have great impact as they unfold across the wall surface.

ABOVE *The fabric bed-hangings and the wallpaper are printed with the same classic toile de Jouy design. Using the same pattern on walls and fabric is an eighteenth-century French practice which has become universally popular among interior designers.*

OPPOSITE *Reproductions of historic wallpapers are often recoloured to look fresh for today's interiors. When they were first introduced, these papers were intended to look like floral fabrics.*

Toile de Jouy

In the eighteenth century, wallpaper designs known as 'toile de Jouy' were originally inspired by the manufacture of printed fabric at Jouy-en-Josas, a little village outside Paris. Here the fabrics were printed on a neutral background, usually in red but sometimes in blue, brown or magenta. The printing technique was unique: at the time it was an astonishing innovation to print fabric using an engraved copper roller. The result was a technique similar to printmaking, but using fabric instead of paper, which gave the engraver the ability to adapt a huge variety of pictures for fabric. One characteristic of toile de Jouy designs is the narrative element: some show shepherds in pastoral pleasures; others take scenes from classical mythology. Motifs from everyday life are often portrayed and the influence of *Chinoiserie* is evident. In English toile the subject matter was simpler, and wallpapers show leaves, birds, flowers and figures, printed in line in a single colour.

Toile de Jouy designs are ideal for coordinated fabric and paper effects, as their single-colour printing and natural background makes them easy on the eye. They make a harmonious and delicate decoration very much in the French style. The finely etched lines of authentic Jouy papers give differing depths of tone and therefore more variety and life to the paper.

Other wallpapers printed to match fabric designs are available but, unlike the monotone effect of toile, they come in several colours. Chintz patterns, for example, have inspired ranges of matching wallpapers and fabrics. Extensive use of a pictorial design can be overpowering, and a wise course is to choose papers, fabrics and borders in coordinating colours but different patterns.

Matching wallpapers and fabrics is not a recent trend. It was popular in the early eighteenth century, when wallpaper makers were often involved in all aspects of interior design. Arts and Crafts and other late-nineteenth-century designers made fabrics and wallpapers to the same patterns. Today, the same idea lies behind manufacturers' coordinated interior ranges.

OPPOSITE *Traditionally depicted in tones of rusty red, the finely drawn motifs in toile de Jouy fabrics print crisply on paper. Manufacturers sometimes produce the same pattern on both paper and fabric, presenting an ideal opportunity to create an integrated design scheme.*

BELOW *A strongly patterned toile de Jouy wallpaper is coordinated with a matching fabric covering the bed and chairs in this attic bedroom in Ireland.*

Decorative drapery

Trompe l'oeil detailing – featuring silky-textured fabrics twisted, draped, swagged, trimmed and tied into bows – was a popular wallpaper theme in the early nineteenth century. Such effects naturally appeared as part of the elaborate floral designs produced by many French manufacturers. Wallpaper as drapery, in the form of decorative borders and separate ornaments, assumed a finishing role in room decoration which is enjoying a resurgence of popularity today.

French wallpapers depicted realistic-looking examples of the elaborate drapery styles then in vogue. Some, for instance, represented life-sized satin curtains, with highlights and shading very skilfully creating the illusion of pleats and folds. They were often trimmed with cords, tassels, and other elaborate passementerie of Empire ornamentation. Others were extravagant creations in lace, luxuriantly draped and finished with little flourishes of frills and scalloped edges. Posies of flowers were added at intervals and – just for good measure – a few ribbons and bows kept the whole design together.

There are reproductions of these opulent French lacy wallpaper designs, and in the right location they can look delightful. Lace wallpaper is so pretty when seen in small pieces that it is easy to fall in love with the idea and fail to visualize its impact *en masse*. Unless the rest of the decoration is suitably restrained, the result can look rather overdone. Instead, for maximum impact, limit the use of this decorative paper to one wall and keep the rest plain.

Easier to use are the simpler versions of trompe l'oeil lace wallpaper, recreated from the very earliest examples, which perfectly capture the lightness and

LEFT *Papers inspired by lace can be dramatic as well as refined. The paper on the floor is a copy of a seventeenth-century design and looks similar to the fine blackwork embroideries of the period.*

OPPOSITE *Wallpaper printed to look like silk drapery creates an astonishing effect in this hallway, its opulence being entirely in keeping with the neo-classical architecture. The folds of fabric seem to be held up by the cornice and drape in sumptuous swathes towards the floor.*

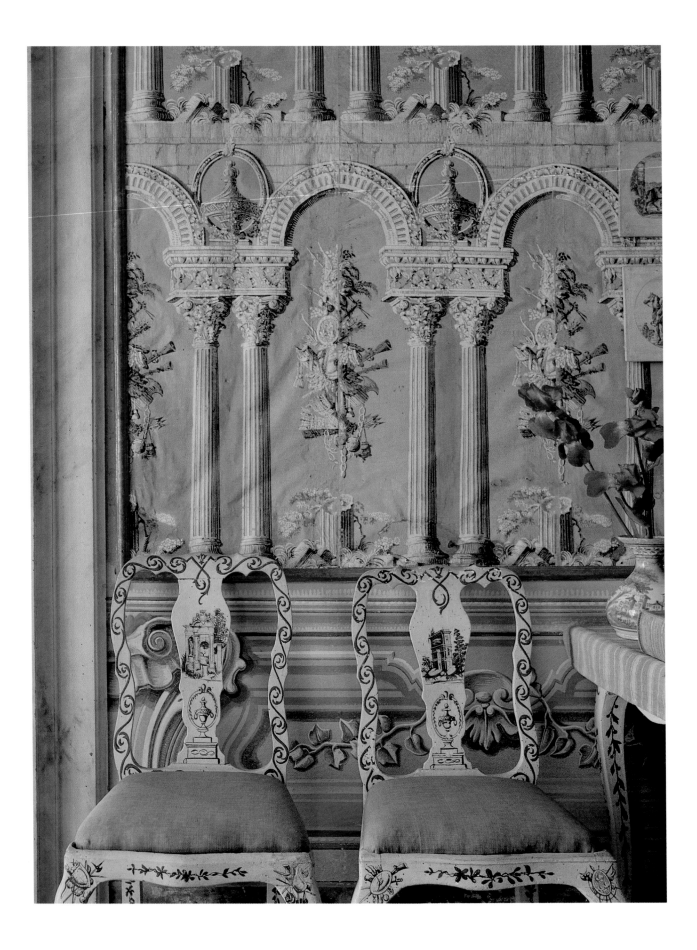

delicacy of lace. The design is printed in white over a coloured ground, so that different tones are created according to the closeness of the pattern. Quite another impression is given when the printing is reversed and a dark pattern is printed on a light background: it looks less like lace, and the overall rhythm of the pattern is predominant.

Elements of architecture

Trompe l'oeil paper effects imitating structural elements of interiors such as pillars, dados and cornices have long been popular among designers for their ability to adjust the apparent proportions of rooms according to favoured principles and to provide just the right finishing framework to more fanciful pictorial and other decorative papers.

In some periods and styles only selected elements are deemed appropriate, like the balustrading effects applied to the dado section of walls adorned with scenic wallpapers, or the deep plasterwork-effect friezes and coffered ceiling designs that became popular in the late nineteenth century.

In periods when neo-classicism has exercised a strong influence, the entire vocabulary of classical ornament has been called into play, with three-dimensional niches and statuary providing focal points on walls enlivened with the illusion of horizontal divisions and vertical columns. Decorating an interior with these architectural elements was a serious business, for the paper hanger had to deploy the relief-effect mouldings and other elements in correct relation to the room's main source of light as well as conforming to strict principles of order and proportion.

The flourish of decorative plasterwork has frequently been imitated in wallpaper. Elaborate Rococo mouldings and *Chinoiserie*-inspired motifs can be seen in historic papers – the scrolls and cartouches formed by the fake plaster often containing little scenes or vignettes. Some designs are more classical in appearance, perhaps reflecting the influence of the superb plaster decoration in the interiors designed by Robert Adam. In Edwardian England delicate papers in plain colours were enlivened with elegant arabesques and ribbons with highly convincing trompe l'oeil plasterwork.

Certain specialist companies still print a repertoire of separate architectural elements such as borders and mouldings, as well as more elaborate motifs such as pilasters and columns, for enterprising decorators to incorporate into room schemes. They range in style from the classical to reinterpretations of the eighteenth-century Gothick style. These elements make it possible to create an illusion of architectural embellishment in a room which is bare of ornamentation. Where there is no cornice, one can be added, either by the simple addition of a trompe l'oeil border – a dentil frieze, an acanthus scroll, or an egg-and-dart border (see page 139) – or any other classical motif and border which will run in a straight line between ceiling and wall. For the more adventurous, there are whole collections of decorative ornaments, printed to look like carved stone or decorative plasterwork, which can be used to conjure up all the romance of a classical room.

A medieval Gothic border with pointed arches and quatrefoil detailing can be used in the same way at the top of the wall to create the illusion of dramatic stone arches. Depending on the colour of the walls and the decoration in the rest of the room the effect may be dark and medieval, or a light reinterpretation of eighteenth-century Gothick architectural style.

OPPOSITE *A small room in this villa in Tuscany is hung with a magnificent eighteenth-century French wallpaper. The three-dimensional effect of the columns and arches is achieved by the contrast of light and shade. Classical trophies hang between the arches.*

BELOW *This modern interpretation of an eighteenth-century theme explores the Gothic vocabulary of architectural ornament rather than the classical. The eye is drawn into a landscape of trompe l'oeil fantasy with follies and castle ruins.*

LEFT *Stone provides a magnificently weighty subject for wallpaper designs. The effect this achieves is usually determined by the treatment of the joins between the blocks. If they look deeply recessed and moulded by light and shade, as in the paper on the rear wall, the effect is massive. When the mortar is indicated by nothing more than a simple line, they are more restrained in impact.*

OPPOSITE *A stone block wallpaper has elegant proportions, making it particularly suitable for hallways where it will create a sense of spaciousness and light.*

Stone block

Fake marbling has been a stock in trade of the painter's craft for centuries, transforming wood and plasterwork to create the illusion of the more expensive material. Wallpapers, too, have been made to resemble various kinds of marble, as well as other masonry, with equal conviction. In the past, stone and marble effects were deemed particularly suitable for hallways, sometimes accompanied by ornate trompe l'oeil architectural elements.

The natural colouring of stone wallpaper is a surprisingly effective background for pictures and its simplicity makes it a perfect foil for furniture. With its clean-cut style it can look particularly good in entrance halls – where the effect of stone blocks creates the impression of space and ordered symmetry. The wall-like illusion of blocks of stone is sometimes quite simply achieved by a grid of pale lines representing mortar. Other papers are more three-dimensional and look like great wedges of smooth hewn stone or ashlar. The impression can be completed with stone flags or tiles on the floor.

Among the most popular *faux* effects in wallpaper today are the papers printed in imitation of marble. At their simplest, marble effects may be little more than an expanse of flat colour broken with just enough light veining to give life to the surface. Really expensive hand-painted marble papers are obviously the most lustrous and convincing because the veining evolves over the paper in exactly the same way as in genuine marble; there is no obvious repeat. Large expanses of marble paper can evoke a rather cool, spartan atmosphere but this can also be used to your advantage when attempting to create the pared-down look associated with many contemporary interiors. Here, the natural appearance of marble, stone or even concrete-effect wallpapers provides an uncomplicated background for a few well-chosen pieces of furniture.

Marble occurs naturally in an enormous variety of colours, but you can also find *faux* marble papers tinted turquoise or other completely artificial colours. It is best to stick to the natural warm tones of Italian marble – rose pink, sienna yellow, ochre, flame, rich dark greens, mellow browns, black veined with grey, grey veined with white, white with grey veining, and every conceivable variation on the same theme. You can also consider combining some of the more realistic stone-effect papers such as the speckled greys of granite with the rich penetrating blue of lapis lazuli or the vivid green gradations of malachite, all of which contrast superbly with the restrained coolness of marbled papers.

Wood grain

Like marbling, fake wood-graining has an honourable pedigree: for centuries people have sought to upgrade the timber of their buildings and furniture to make it resemble the fashionable wood of the moment – oak, mahogany, rosewood, even bamboo. In the eighteenth and nineteenth centuries wood-effect wallpaper designs, combed by hand or block-printed, imitated wainscoting and carved wood panelling. They were often intended for dados, and, as with other architectural papers, were much advocated for hallways. Using different panels it was possible to build up quite complex arrangements of dados, cornices, pillars, and panelling in between. Trompe l'oeil techniques could create the illusion of relief carvings and mouldings. Some French nineteenth-century papers were designed to frame scenic papers with the effect of wooden architectural elements, allowing the landscape in the panorama to dissolve into the distance. Popular in Germany at the same time were wallpapers which imitated a kind of 'hunting lodge' decorative style, depicting dark wood with heavily carved columns and niches – some with carved trophies of dead game arranged within them.

A number of traditional designs are still in production today, and panelled papers with dados, or even dados themselves, can bring a touch of grandeur in the appropriate setting. Modern wood-effect papers are far less ornate and fit easily into contemporary settings. Some simply resemble planks – not necessarily the ubiquitous pine-strip panelling but wider boards with an interesting grain and realistic-looking raised finish. Pale colours grained with grey, reminiscent of driftwood, give a pretty, light, panelled effect; mellower tones with the warmth of natural wood evoke a 'back to the country' feel.

Wood grain wallpaper looks most realistic when you are unaware of the repeat pattern: the same grain markings occurring endlessly up the wall do not convey the feel of natural wood. Most wood grain paper manufacturers solve this by keeping the design simple, and some of the best papers work well in simulation of painted tongue-and-groove boards. When wood grain papers are pasted on the wall to dado height and topped with a border, they achieve a fashionable look in a bathroom or a hallway for a fraction of the cost of wood. More expensive

OPPOSITE *Paper with a realistic wood-effect looks as if the walls have been lined with driftwood found on the beach. Paper like this is useful when a natural look is desired.*

papers sometimes appear almost three-dimensional in their textured surface. Broad white-washed planks look effective in a room with light furnishings and some are so convincingly trompe l'oeil that it is impossible to tell that they are not wood. Other papers achieve effects of colour-washed wood. Wood grain wallpaper can be hung to look like planks in contemporary style, or, with the addition of panel borders, an illusion of a panelled room can be designed.

The garden-room effect

Wallpapers imitating trelliswork and bamboo appear to pierce the wall's surface, taking the eye through to an apparent space behind the grid of bamboo, stone, fretwork or garden trelliswork and so creating a delightful airy feeling. Stone-effect trelliswork creates a light and delicate atmosphere. Green trelliswork, or a fretwork that looks like wood can bring a fresh, conservatory-like atmosphere to a dark room, particularly when partnered with real plants and fresh flowers.

Many trellis designs have traditionally been used as dado papers, and this provides an opportunity for combining two patterned papers. Classically, a bamboo trellis or a fretwork design will complement Chinese-style papers and build up a distinctive theme for a room. A more contemporary mood is achieved by using a garden trelliswork paper as a dado with a plain paper above.

Trelliswork is also the inspiration for hundreds of geometric wallpapers. Designed as flat patterns without the three-dimensional element, they vary in scale from the tiniest diamonds – which hardly register as a pattern when seen from a distance – to large, bold outlines. While these patterns can look simple and attractive in the

OPPOSITE *A simple trellis design is traced by intertwined leaves creating the light and airy feel of a summer garden.*

LEFT *Wallpaper printed in imitation of split bamboo has a realistically three-dimensional appearance. It gives the surface texture in a natural setting.*

small swatch of a pattern book, once they are hung on the wall, the geometry may take on another character and form completely different shapes, perhaps moving in long intersecting diagonal lines or enclosing the room in a cage-like grid. It may be wise to try out a large sample of the design before making a purchase so that you have a good idea of the finished look.

Paint effects

The time-honoured distressed paint finishes that have recently become so successful as a decorating fashion have been perfectly imitated in wallpaper designs. Wallpaper versions of popular paint techniques such as dragging and ragging, splattering and sponging, and many other processes with vigorous-sounding names all make pleasant, subtly textured wall surfaces without the anxiety and effort of doing it yourself with messy paint, pigment, and glaze. Paint-effect papers have an added advantage; you can see what the result will be before you start, thus eliminating the risk involved in experimenting with unfamiliar techniques and applications, which require skill and practise. Wallpaper solves these problems and lets you choose paint effects which you might never attempt if you were doing it yourself. Fresco, for example, looks enticingly rough and ancient when it is applied by a skilful painter, but anyone can be assured of perfect results by choosing a fresco-effect wallpaper.

Stencilling

When the earliest wallpapers were printed only in black, stencilling was one way of adding any additional colours required. This traditional form of wall decoration has influenced wallpaper designs in a number of ways, both in the types of pattern produced and in the textural quality of the painted colour on paper.

Many of the wallpaper and border designs that pre-date World War I were based on stencilling, with their pools of bright jewel-like colours inside thickly drawn black outlining. The spectacular wide friezes of the eminent Art Nouveau wallpaper designer William Shand Kydd made a dramatic design statement around a room, with bold motifs filling large lengths of wall space.

Skilled artists and craftsmen are producing hand-stencilled wallpaper today but since the method is time-consuming, the results are expensive. However, it is a style well-suited to mechanical reproduction and many designs are based on the effects created by stencil techniques.

Some of the prettiest stencil designs available now are the simplest repeated patterns, running like stripes up the wall. This is most likely a modern interpretation of hand-stencilling on wooden walls, where the painted wooden planks formed a ready-made framework for the design of wide vertical bands. Decorating the walls with simple stencilled motifs was popular in rural communities in Scandinavia and in eighteenth-century America, when it was difficult to obtain wallpaper. The charming patterns from these sources have provided ongoing inspiration for designers. With the revival of interest in the simple, country-style interiors of Scandinavian and early American origin, stencilled and stencil-effect wallpapers, which are both charming in their simplicity and easy to live with, have enjoyed a renewed vogue. These wallpapers look especially good in bedrooms, where the simplicity of stencilled designs offers a fresh, light appeal.

OPPOSITE *Stencil designs are among the simplest ways to decorate the wall. Here an understated stripe pattern is formed by a repeated S-shaped scroll, intertwined with the paper.*

BELOW *The popular paint effect of fresco can be achieved very successfully in wallpaper, without the effort and mess of paint.*

simple pattern

Of all the different wallpaper styles a flat repeating pattern of flowers printed on paper designed to hang from wall to ceiling, wall to wall, is the image which occurs to most people when wallpaper is mentioned. Easily the largest volume of patterned wallpapers produced falls into this category. The underlying principle of all patterns is to make an overall decoration with an unobtrusively repeating motif. The elements may be small and subtle, bold and eyecatching – or anything in between.

A simple repeat pattern may 'read' from a distance as a series of regularly spaced dots or motifs, a diagonally based arrangement, an all-over floral motif, a stripe, or a continuous interweaving effect. Pronounced colour contrasts will make the elements stand out; close gradations of colour or tone in the design have a far gentler effect.

Many of the patterns available to us today are authentic reproductions of old designs, often copied from small fragments found in old houses. But often designs and motifs are reproduced – or adapted and reinterpreted – without particular reference to their earlier incarnation, and when you choose a wallpaper from a pattern book you do not necessarily know its antecedents. Much of the vocabulary of pattern is traditional, emerging again and again in new guises. And every so often a new language of pattern emerges, such as the highly articulated appreciation of flat, two-dimensional design that emerged in English wallpapers dating from the second half of the last century.

Floral designs

Among the most popular patterns of all wallpaper designs are floral papers, and there is consequently an infinite variety of styles from which to choose. Flowers are a quintessentially English theme in decoration, beloved in both country and town houses. It probably reflects the English love affair with gardens, and choosing fabrics and wallpapers with a floral motif is a way of taking the pleasures of the garden inside the home. Flower patterns vary from the simplest single flower, repeated like a tiny dot all over the wall, to huge blowsy roses gathered in lush bunches to make a lavish all-over pattern. Some wallpapers replicate individual flowers in almost botanical accuracy; others are uncompromisingly stylized, using the flower as a basis to create attractive colours and shapes on the paper.

Many designs are based on archive reproductions, because floral motifs have a long and successful history in wallpaper, each generation reinterpreting nature in the style which captures the spirit of the age. Art Nouveau, Art Deco, and Arts and Crafts are each instantly recognizable, while differing totally from the rather prim flowers of Georgian wallpapers or the bulbous, showy floral designs beloved by the Victorians.

Historically, wallpaper printing techniques tended not to allow soft gradations of colour and the different tones had to be conveyed in hard-edged flat areas of colour. This meant that considerable skill was required by the designer to interpret the subtle shades in petals, leaves, and stamens and create an effective result. But new methods of printing can now produce an almost photographic interpretation which often brings a freshness and delicacy that wallpapers previously lacked.

ABOVE *'Berkeley Sprig', a simple repeating bell-flower motif on a diagonal ground, suggests the stitched look of antique quilts. This paper was copied from a fragment found during the renovation of an eighteenth-century house in Berkeley Square, London.*

OPPOSITE *A petal from one of the peonies on the left-hand paper makes a delicate pattern for the paper on the right. The two are designed to work together, giving the opportunity for some variety in scale and pattern.*

Leaves and foliage

Second only to flowers in popularity, leaf motifs are freely used as a design inspiration in wallpaper. Anything from carefully drawn studies of ferns and grasses to bold swirling patterns of the classical acanthus leaf. Branches of leaves which climb up wallpapers in waving tendrils are similar in spirit to antique Chinese wallpapers, or Indian 'Tree of Life' designs. Very successful, too, are wallpapers created to look like medieval knot gardens, with interlacing paths linking like strapwork and clipped hedges and borders. Topiary trees cut into fantastical shapes have also inspired designers to create interesting wallpapers and borders. Many of these designs have in common the natural colour combination of white and green. It is a tried-and-tested formula, always popular because it looks fresh, is easy to live with, and lightens up dark spaces. Not that it is essential to be true to nature in colours. Some of the most original designs take the form of a leaf as inspiration and interpret it in a whole palette of colours other than green. The leaf design opposite is printed in lavender – a colour not normally associated with leaves – and the leaf wallpaper design on page 88 is printed in 22-carat gold leaf.

Botanical prints make good subjects for both leaf and flower wallpapers. They are beautifully drawn and their delicate colourings can be very well reproduced on paper. The effect is amazingly three-dimensional. Sometimes the wallpaper looks as if it has been printed with complete pages taken from an ancient botanical book – almost as if the pages have been pasted to the wall. It creates a design similar to that of an eighteenth-century print room, where prints were pasted directly to the wall on a coloured background (see page 159).

Clusters of herbs with their great variety of leaf shapes – rosemary, thyme, marjoram, mint, sage, basil and all the other aromatic plants from the herb garden – make delightful subjects for wallpapers and add an almost aromatic atmosphere to a kitchen.

Ferns and bracken are classics in the design vocabulary of both wallpapers and fabrics. The lines of their curling fronds inspire designers over and over again, every designer reinterpreting the leaf in a unique way, so that in one design you may see a botanically perfect fern leaf depicted in the natural freshness of early spring, while in another the fern leaf becomes a loose shadow, a misty gauze-like illusion in white, softly printed on a gentle background colour.

The immense variety of shapes found in leaves lend themselves to free interpretation. The French Post-Impressionist painter Matisse was a pioneer of this form. He cut out the shapes of fig leaves, freehand so that their long leafy 'fingers' were exaggerated into quite different forms. He then pasted the cut-outs onto the wall to form murals in a mixture of bright primary colours, and softer pinks, purples and greens. The result was a highly dramatic visual statement of such force that designers and artists have been inspired by his example to experiment in the same way. The freely interpreted oak leaf paper, shown opposite, was created using Matisse's work as a starting point. The crisply shaped leaves are coloured in a way far removed from nature, but many successful designs borrow shapes from natural sources and recolour them to work in contemporary decoration. This paper is unusual, too, in that it breaks the convention of the repeated image in wallpaper. Drops do not to match up side to side but are hung and reverse-hung in sequence, with the joins made at random, so that the overall effect is of leaves tumbling over the wall in no rhythm. It makes a refreshing change from the predictable repeat which chacterizes most papers.

ABOVE *The pretty topiary trees on the wallpaper and the intricate design of box-tree hedges replicate the patterns of medieval knot gardens. Combined with the wood-panelled dado, they bring an outdoor look to the decoration.*

OPPOSITE *A stylized oak leaf swirls over this paper, its contemporary image highlighted by the originality of the colour. Leaves need not always be green in wallpaper patterns.*

ABOVE *A starry night-sky wallpaper captures the moment when the sun has just set and the sky still glows with reflected warmth.*

OPPOSITE *Airy clouds drifting across walls and ceiling create a romantic atmosphere in this bedroom.*

Clouds patterns

Wallpaper patterns depicting light, airy clouds floating across a summer sky create a dreamy effect, especially when they are applied to the ceiling and walls of the bedroom or bathroom. It is immensely relaxing to lie in bed or the bath and gaze upwards into a peaceful design of sky and clouds.

The practice of papering and painting the ceiling with sky and clouds is not new. The great Italian Renaissance masters of trompe l'oeil painting, such as Tiepolo and Veronese, perfected the art of painting ceilings in which the sky seems to fade into the distance. It is as though the spectator on the ground is looking up through a hole in the ceiling to see the heavens beyond, where the clouds float in infinite space. Tiepolo populated his skies with activity – chariots drawn by galloping horses race across the sky, as masterful gods and goddesses look on, and groups of cherubs play among the fluffy clouds. All of this imagery is fantastically grandiose for today's interiors, but the essence of the idea – the clouds in a summer sky – and the sense of light and space are worth pursuing.

This freehand spirit in wallpaper is impossible to achieve using the mechanical wallpaper printing process, as identical clouds are repeated every 60cm (24in) or so. To produce a cloud pattern that is constantly changing, and made up of different diaphanous shapes, one has to turn to hand-printed wallpaper designs.

The wallpaper shown opposite is ingeniously designed so that all the clouds look different over quite a large area of wall. The effect is achieved by using two rolls of paper, each hand-printed with slightly different cloud formations. Every cloud on both rolls will join up with any other cloud, thus allowing the possibility of a large variety in cloud shapes. The finished effect is magical, and the paper works well hung on both walls and ceilings. Papering the ceiling will bring an element of surprise to the decoration, for it is far more usual to paint the ceiling plain white and leave it at that. In fact, the ceiling is the one large undecorated area in most rooms, so a cloud wallpaper is the perfect choice where such informality is appropriate.

Night sky

Daytime can give way to night and change the mood. The same paper recoloured to look like the evening sky gives a quite different effect. The blue is much richer – a warm sapphire blue, with great depth. It captures the colour before the light from the sun has completely disappeared and the night sky becomes inky blue. The clouds have that iridescent lustre which is the reflection of the final rays of light, or even the reflection of an early moon, and the paper is sprinkled with dozens of tiny gold and silver stars which capture and reflect the light. A wallpaper like this hung on the walls or the ceiling of a dining room, where the candlelight is reflected in the sparkling stars, makes for a romantic atmosphere.

A simple star-studded paper can have a similar effect, and there are dozens of wallpapers which use the star as their key design motif. Sometimes the stars are printed on the paper in a regular pattern, so that from a distance they form an elegant grid of spiky dots. On other wallpapers the stars are more random, creating the effect of stars scattered over the paper in a way which gives them a more celestial appearance.

Classic striped wallpapers

Stripes are a special sort of flat pattern. Striped designs have a most remarkable versatility and can add a striking elegance to a wide variety of settings. The effect of the stripe design can vary depending on whether the stripes are presented as a close arrangement of matt and shiny textures in the same colour, a muted stripe in subtle colours, or very broad vertical bands in strong contrasting colours. The width and the colour of the stripe control the impact of the design. Very narrow stripes will blend into one another from a distance and appear more like a textured surface. Broad vertical stripes, on the other hand, are visually arresting wherever they are hung. A bold stripe design may fill the entire width of the wallpaper, with just a slim border running down one side. This hardly looks like a stripe in the sample book, but hung on the wall it reveals its pronounced vertical divisions.

The character of a striped wallpaper and its decorative effect is decided much more by the combination of colours than in the arrangement or width of the stripes. A pale colour looks attractive alternating with white, and imparts a fresh, sunny, informal look, which works well as a background to light wood, cane, or painted pieces of furniture. A mixture of strong, deep colours will produce a richer, more sophisticated effect and is a wonderful background for mahogany and oak. A closely toned combination of stripes provides an excellent background for pictures and furniture, while strongly contrasting stripes make such an impact that they may detract from, rather than enhance, objects displayed against them.

Stripes are one kind of wallpaper in which hand-printing does not promise a superior product. Neither the woodblock technique nor screen-printing are particularly suitable for producing long straight lines, because every time the

LEFT *A fresh blue-and-white stripe paper has an almost tent-like effect in this light and sunny room. The classic stripe is given a contemporary twist by the more detailed border running along the top.*

OPPOSITE *A classic Regency stripe in ochre, red and cream is an appropriate choice for this traditional setting. Stopping the paper at dado level and painting the moulding adds a strong horizontal to balance the proportions of the room.*

block or screen is printed there is a chance of misalignment and a consequent
wobble where the lines join. Before the use of mechanical production methods
these papers were made with a long V-shaped trough which was divided into
sections with slots at the base. The paint was poured into the trough and the
paper pulled through underneath. Modern manufacturing techniques are much
faster. Also, since the design element in a stripe is so basic, very inexpensive
papers can look just as effective as expensive ones – there is no need for
extravagance in making an attractive decoration, although more exclusive ranges
may have more subtlety and sophistication in their colourings.

Stripes have the great advantage of being relatively timeless, which means
that the decoration will not date, unlike some patterns which can look very *passé*
after a few years. Nor do stripes impose a particular style on a room, demanding,
for instance, a country living feel or a collection of precious antique furniture.

Many of the more decorative striped patterns were originally copied from
textiles, and the mixture of the stripe interspersed with other patterns like flowers
produces a much softer feel – more akin to fabric. Some moirés are produced as
stripes, giving a combination of sheen and matt in the most understated patterns.
Some reproduce the effect of taffeta or watered silk stripes. Wallpaper designs
taken from ethnic woven fabrics – Indian ikat designs and brilliantly coloured
stripes from Asia and North Africa – are rich and effectively colourful. Hung on the

LEFT *This clever stripe design graduates slowly in colour to a strong central blue. The colour fusion gives movement to the design. The same striped theme is picked up in the fabric used to upholster the chair.*

walls and taken up over the ceiling, they can create the effect of a sumptuously hung Bedouin tent.

Striped rooms with the wallpaper continued onto the ceiling were popular in Regency England and Napoleonic France; indeed, the fashion cropped up all over Europe. The effect was of a campaign tent, where everything, including the furniture, had to be instantly transportable. It was a classic example of current events – the Napoleonic wars – affecting contemporary taste. Rooms like this are easy to copy using striped papers in brisk military colours – rich reds, Prussian blues, dark greens, or greys – and finishing them off with rope borders to add to the illusion. The furniture can be chosen to complement the style – plain dark furniture, imposing lamps, antique rugs on the wooden floor, and curtains hung from poles with arrowheads and quivers as finials, in true Napoleonic style.

Rooms decorated with so-called Regency stripes take on an air of elegant formality. Hallways are particularly suited to striped wallpaper either from wall to ceiling, or contrasting with a plain dado. In any room where the feeling of height needs to be increased, stripes will help visually to heighten the ceiling.

Contemporary striped wallpaper

Turning a stripe on its side gives it an instant contemporary lift. Horizontal stripes (see page 8 and opposite) suddenly look more exciting than the conventional floor-to-ceiling variety. It is not too difficult to hang wallpaper along the length of the wall, rather than from top to bottom. Of course the lengths are much longer so care needs to be taken when the paper is loosely folded ready to hang (see page 169), and a spirit level is an essential piece of equipment. Bear in mind that the look will be spoiled if the lines appear to be sloping down the wall or, even worse, converging on each other.

Not all striped papers look good hanging horizontally. Narrow striped designs appear distinctly odd when hung in this way. In fact, as a general rule the wider the stripe the better it looks. A 25cm (10in) width is best, while a width of less than12cm (5in) appears meagre. Another hanging technique is to run the entire width of wallpaper horizontally and then hang the same wallpaper in a different colour above and below, thus creating your own unique stripe. But be careful with your colour choice – too much contrast may be difficult to live with. It is better to choose two colours of the same tone or one colour in a lighter and a darker shade.

Curves, dots and circles

Curling wallpaper patterns can produce an effect similar to check designs (see page 102) – the regularly repeated pattern becomes like a grid giving a rigid structure to the overall design. When the curves are drawn with graphic precision the result is a quite mechanical high-tech look demanding an exacting level of perfection in every aspect of the interior decoration. Geometric wallpaper like this creates an environment for steel and chrome objects and furniture, with natural wood, concrete, and rubber to complement its sharp urban styling.

Dots placed at regular intervals over the paper can have a cheery polka-dot appearance and wallpapers using dots as their motif can be as zany as the colours they are printed in. Vibrant primaries seem to bounce off the wall but dots coloured in honey, butter, cream and beige will, as always with these shades, have a much more restrained presence.

Loose curves make for a softer, more feminine look, still with a contemporary edge but gentler in effect, and probably easier for most people to live with.

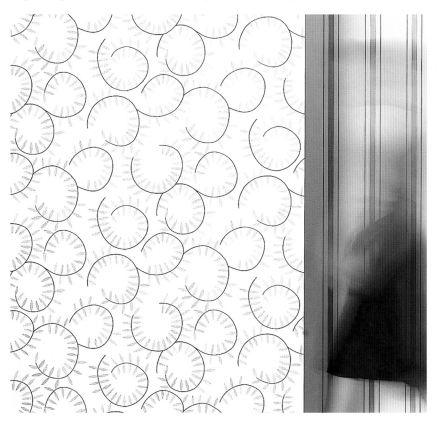

LEFT *The softly drawn curves in this imaginative design seem to crawl around the wall like 'hairy caterpillars' and give a sensation of movement to the wallpaper.*

OPPOSITE *Circles drawn with modern precision make a design like cuts of steel tubing. Here the wallpaper is printed in two different sizes, giving the drama of scale to the decoration.*

contemporary papers

innovative designs

Until recently wallpaper has been a very conventional medium. Many designs are archive reproductions, or adapted from motifs whose popularity has stood the test of time. Established printing methods have dictated the repetitive image which is seen as the dominant feature of wallpaper. But now a small number of designers are changing the way we look at wallpaper and challenging our perceptions of what we can hang on our walls. Often this has meant casting aside old ideas. Whereas generations of students were taught how to step and repeat patterns in order to make wallpapers suitable for printing in industrial quantities, contemporary wallpaper designers have rejected this concept of the repeated image in favour of the freedom to design much looser motifs on a large scale.

ABOVE *The slow process of hand-printing allows time for a rich depth of colour to build up on these striped wallpapers. Although old printing skills are used, the colour palette is lively and up-to-date.*

OPPOSITE *A very broad stripe offers a contemporary twist on an old favourite. The wide horizontal divisions in this wallpaper are separated by thin gold lines. These reflect the light and create a subtle shimmer which gives life to the wallpaper design.*

PREVIOUS PAGE *Complementary papers hung on adjacent walls define the seating and eating areas in this modern, open-plan interior.*

Many wallpaper designs in current production draw on traditional patterns and motifs so that although they are contemporary in one sense, they still rely on the past. For example, many of the popular damask patterns, Regency stripes, trelliswork and arabesques available are replicas of old wallpapers seen hanging in historical houses. Flower motifs, perhaps the most popular of images, belong among the thousands of traditional wallpaper designs which have stood the test of time.

But modern wallpaper can also be contemporary in the cutting-edge, state-of-the-art sense. These innovative papers belong to the designers who strive to take a fresh approach and create wallpapers which, in the future, will make a statement about the prevailing style of our own decade.

New interpretations of traditional themes

Stripes are among the most classic of all wallpaper designs, and are always popular because they bring a crisp and tailored finish to any room. Normal practice is to hang striped wallpaper vertically on the wall, but it does not take much to bring a contemporary edge to a traditional stripe. A broad striped wallpaper hung horizontally instead of vertically immediately appears fresh and interesting. It creates a good background for modern pieces of furniture, but because it is so simple, it will also give an up-to-date look to a room furnished with antique pieces. Subtle variations of colour or different tones of the same colour work better than sharp contrasts, which have a rather dazzling effect.

Many contemporary versions of traditional designs take their theme from ethnic or tribal motifs. Ideas which stem originally from sources as geographically diverse as North Africa, Mexico, Peru and India are adapted from wall hangings, rugs, fabrics, tiles and painted wall decorations. Reproduced on wallpaper in the sun-baked colours of their native countries they seem to add an exotic air of heat and spices to modern decoration.

Traditional Chinese and Japanese designs are enjoying great popularity in the 'East meets West' style of decoration. Designs based on calligraphy have an interesting linear quality which makes them fairly easy to translate into wallpaper design. Printed to simulate the appearance of black ink on parchment, these papers work well when combined with a range of pale neutrals from ivory, cream, beige and taupe down to sophisticated browns and blacks.

Medieval inspiration

We are also very familiar with Gothic motifs and medieval patterns which inspired the repeat wallpaper patterns of William Morris and the Arts and Crafts movement (see page 28). Tudor roses and Fleur-de-lys, for example, are often the inspiration for contemporary wallpapers, and when they are handled lightly in up-to-date colourings it is easy to see why their charm is so widely appreciated.

Floral patterns

Traditionally flowers and leaves have formed a huge vocabulary of motifs for wallpaper design, just as they have in fabric, but now grasses and herbs – plants that reflect our current concern for a natural environment – are becoming increasingly popular in contemporary designs. Their appeal derives from their natural simplicity and their associations with outdoor living as well as their ability to create a delicate, light-filled atmosphere. Some floral wallpapers actually incorporate pieces of dried flower and leaf material in their manufacture – creating a texture similar to handmade gift wrapping paper – that is integral to the paper rather than a flat design printed on top. When decorating interiors with floral papers, choose simple furniture in natural wood or painted, French-style furniture. Together they will create a relaxed ambience which needs only a few fresh flowers in a vase for embellishment.

RIGHT *Fleur-de-lys is such a popular historical motif that it keeps reappearing in different guises on contemporary wallpapers. This is a softly coloured interpretation with an undemanding presence. Available in different colours, it will add surface interest to the walls.*

OPPOSITE *The fragile delicacy of cow parsley is the inspiration for both these loosely designed floral papers. The cow parsley flowerhead in the paper hung on the right-hand side is given a more stylized treatment, marking a subtle difference between the two designs.*

Innovative methods of wallpaper production

New pattern-making techniques have increased the opportunities for designers to produce imaginative wallpaper designs which, at first glance, do not appear to have any visible repeat. The tyranny of the repeated motif in printed wallpaper is one of the most inhibiting factors for a designer, so a pattern which appears to unfold randomly around the room – the leaf design shown below or the clouds paper (see page 69) – seems more closely associated with hand-painted papers or mural decoration than traditional wallpaper printing.

To achieve the effect of a hand-painted room, two rolls of wallpaper are printed with slightly different designs – the same idea, but realized in a slightly different rhythm – and then the papers are hung alternately. The overall effect is of a design which seems to be ever-changing rather than always repeating around the room. Of course, since this paper is printed there is actually a repeat on each drop. Even screen-printing very large designs down each drop of paper cannot prevent the same area being printed several times on a single roll, but since the eye travels sideways – rather than up or down in narrow bands – it will take in the whole effect, so the pattern repeat is never noticed. It is a visual illusion, but one that works for many different kinds of design, opening up the possibility of creating a different style of decoration.

OPPOSITE *Continuous wavy lines weave their way up this paper to produce an effect similar to reeds or grasses growing in the wild. The metallic design is a new take on the traditional stripe, and its light-reflective quality creates a feeling of movement similar to shadows dancing on a wall.*

BELOW *A series of leafy stems curve their way up the surface in this contemporary leaf design. The appearance of fine brushstrokes and the lack of an apparent repeat in the design makes you believe the design has been hand-painted by an artist, rather than printed on paper.*

light-reflective papers

Wonderful effects can be achieved by wallpapers designed to reflect and refract the light as it hits the surface of the wall. Metallic inks and colours incorporating mica give different levels of light reflection. Success lies in the right balance between matt and reflective areas. Many designs contrast shiny areas with others giving a soft glow on a matt ground, thus giving depth to the design.

ABOVE *A stainless steel breakfast bar fixed to the wall of this kitchen has a wallpaper behind it printed with reflective squares, which gives emphasis to its cool, clean lines.*

OPPOSITE *Sharp, modern wallpapers printed with areas of light-reflecting colour contrast with the matt surface of the backgrounds.*

These fabulous contemporary papers change according to the way light plays upon the surface, making them a far more interactive wall decoration than plain paper. For example, areas of the wall where the light hits the surface will sparkle brightly, while other areas not lit by direct light may seem more muted. The kind of light will affect the design too – direct sunlight will enable a metallic design to glisten, while indirect daylight has a softer effect. Artificial light coming from various other directions in the room will reflect different areas, once again changing the atmosphere of the room.

Light-reflective paper production

The most brilliant reflective surface is achieved either with foil or with metallic inks, but a more resonant sheen results from the use of mica mixed into coloured ink. Mica is a mineral which is mined and then ground down to a fine powder-like talc. The mica powder particles catch the light and make the surface glow with a deep lustre. Depending on the nature of the design, mica can give the wallpaper a silky appearance, as if the design was printed on a background of raw silk, or it can be used to give the warm glow of polished pewter. In combination with coloured inks, mica can offer a pearlized finish to a metallic design which seems to rise out of the flat background. When designers use mica in conjunction with a silvery ink, papers look as if they are made from sheets of stainless steel. But if the process is reversed and a design is printed on top of a metallic background, the motif seems to have a life independent of its background. With the vast array of effects that can be created using different combinations of metallic inks and mica, the finished result is determined by the demands of the design and the intentions of the designer.

These greys, silvers, polished steel and pewter colours present a very contemporary feel, but this should not necessarily limit their use to a minimalist interior. Carefully chosen, they will also add an air of sophistication to a more conventional room with its cornice and fireplace, provided that the rest of the colourings in the room are in harmony.

Hanging metallic papers

Papers like this often need careful hanging because mica can come off the surface. It may also mark. Greasy fingers can present a problem, as can paste oozing out from the edges and not being wiped off properly. This should be done very gently before it dries, so no intense rubbing is necessary. On the other hand there are some metallic wallpapers which are very tough, so it is important to discover the paper's resilience from the outset. For areas subject to heavy traffic or wear and tear, such as a family hallway, choose one of the tougher metallic papers, reserving the more delicate papers for less frequently used areas.

Choosing a suitable location

Papers which capture and reflect the light are now produced in such a great variety of designs that it is not difficult to find something which will suit almost any decorating scheme. It is not just contemporary designs which use reflective inks and micas – traditional paper designs use the same materials in their manufacture to introduce surface variation to the pattern. The most restrained designs are those which have two tones of the same colour, one heightened with mica to give it reflection and the other matt. This use of reflective ingredients creates a very subtle effect and a serene atmosphere for a bedroom. Incorporated within a traditional damask paper design (see page 46), the subtle light-changing quality of mica can exactly imitate the way a damask silk weave reflects the light. Printed on a grand scale, a damask design will look very appropriate in a large hallway or sitting room, where the scale of the design can be appreciated. Even a small amount of metallic ink will animate a conventional striped wallpaper and give it unexpected moments of sparkle at intervals along the wall. But, used more boldly, the effect is more dramatic and calls for a room which can take a powerful statement, like a dining room or hallway. Sometimes it is enough simply to hang the metallic-striped paper on one wall only, using just plain paper on the others. This will draw attention to the design without overpowering the room.

OPPOSITE *A wavy line in creamy white is hand-blocked on to the silvery background of this unique paper. The use of traditional nineteenth-century techniques (see page 26) give a rare handcrafted quality to this contemporary design, which combines the best of old and new.*

BELOW *A series of bold metallic horizontal stripes creates the effect of silver streaks as they run through a deep blue background paper. Light-reflective stripes make the walls sparkle in the warm glow of the dining room fire and candlelit table.*

Gilded walls

Most special of all are the papers that are handmade using the real elements of gold leaf, white gold, or silver leaf. These wallpapers are simple in design, but the gilded paper surface gives the walls a shimmering richness which cannot be surpassed. Nothing is as lustrous as real 22-carat gold. It glows with a richness which can never be equalled by metallic paint. Real gold has a depth and warmth which envelops and cossets the room. It captures and reflects the light with radiance and brilliance, and for this reason gold leaf in decoration has to be used with sensitivity and discretion. Traditionally used in small quantities, for instance on picture frames or the gilded wood of antique chairs, gold leaf on wallpaper can be dramatically overpowering. It is important not to overdo it. Just one wall decorated in this way is often enough.

Gold leaf is produced in wafer-thin 12cm (4in) squares of beaten gold, so light that the merest whisper of breath will waft the square into the air, crumpling it into a fraction of its former size. Furniture gilders traditionally work with gold leaf on a little suede pad with a shield to protect it from drafts. They cut it into pieces and apply it to the surface with a sable paintbrush. Easier to use is transfer gold leaf, where the same thin square is held on a backing of tissue until it is in place. Wallpaper using gold leaf has to be created by hand, each square painstakingly positioned on the paper, and then burnished to emphasize its lustre.

RIGHT *The leaf pattern on this wallpaper has been delicately hand-blocked in 22-carat gold leaf. The design catches and reflects the light and will retain its lustre for years to come.*

OPPOSITE *Squares of 22-carat gold are placed irregularly on a background of scarlet, which peeps through at the edges, emphasizing the richness of this luxurious wallpaper.*

Contrasting panels of pattern

The conventional way of hanging wallpaper is wall to wall, ceiling to floor, all the way round the room, and clearly with most wallpapers this is the rational approach. But there are some situations, and indeed some wallpapers, where an alternative arrangement is preferable.

In the 1950s, there was a fashion for hanging one wallpaper on three walls of a room and a different design on the fourth as a way to make you focus on the wallpaper, much as strategic placement of a picture can create a focus. This can still be effective but it does have to be a clearly intentional design decision, and should not look as if the wallpapering is not quite finished. The two designs need to be chosen carefully to complement one another. Using a bold motif on one wall, combined with plain coloured paper on the others (in the same colour as the background of the bold paper), is an effective device. It throws the design into prominence without dominating the room.

Wallpaper hung as a panel can also look very effective contrasting with plain walls papered in a different colour. It concentrates the eye on the wallpaper design whether it is simple or complex, and gives it the importance of a picture.

RIGHT *Two contrasting wallpapers hung in the same bedroom work because both papers are united in the simplicity of their designs and colour scheme.*

OPPOSITE *Panels of squared wallpaper make a bold contrast with the white background of the painted walls.*

texture in paper

There was a time when the idea of textured wallpaper conjured up an image of woodchip – that ubiquitous crack-covering wallpaper which is used to hide uneven wall surfaces. New textured wallpapers owe nothing to this old workhorse and are crisply changing the look of contemporary interiors, producing schemes whose appeal lies in the variety of natural colour and texture.

ABOVE *A basket-weave wallpaper gives an interesting surface texture with its variations of light and shade within the regularity of the weave.*

OPPOSITE *Here, tobacco-coloured hessian (burlap) wallpaper provides a robust textured background for an individual collection of objects. The hessian creates a sense of warmth and harmony in the room, blending with the natural wood table while providing some contrast with the metal objects arranged on it.*

Recent trends in wallpaper are showing signs of a revival of interest in textured papers which appeal as much to the tactile sensations as they do to the eye. Even that old sixties standby hessian (burlap) is getting a reappraisal. Available in natural colours of beige, stone, taupe and cream, hessian looks attractive in simple modern interiors, blending well with light wood floors, the clean lines of contemporary furniture and simply hung curtains in natural woven materials.

Grass paper has a similar appeal. Its texture is enhanced by the different thicknesses of each blade of grass which create a horizontal rhythm across the wall surface. Some of these natural grass papers achieve a rougher, more rustic texture when pieces of bark and leaves are woven in with the grasses. They make a lively background for informal rooms and work well with ethnic furniture in dark wood, richly coloured fabrics, and handwoven rugs.

Raffia papers are equally successful when combined with this earthy style of decoration, and create a beautiful basket-weave pattern on the wall, impossible to achieve with paint. Some Japanese wallpaper manufacturers have taken this basket-weave texture a step further. To create a sophisticated weave, they lay thin slivers of wood on to a paper backing and then interlay the wood as though it were parquet flooring.

Imitation papers

Other interesting textural effects have been created with papers which look as though they have been soaked in water, crumpled up and then pasted to the wall. In reality, this effortless-looking finish has been painstakingly constructed as wallpaper and hung in strips like conventional papers. The final result can look completely random, like crushed paper bags on a huge scale. In other papers the look is more structured, with concertina folds of paper pressed together to make ridges that resemble a Fortuny dress.

At the other end of the textural scale are papers fabricated to look like concrete – a refined form of industrial chic which lends itself to spacious loft living, large public places and reception areas. It is a sophisticated urban look requiring an environment of steel, chrome, hard floors, large windows and, above all, space: roughly textured paper is not designed for a small domestic room or a narrow hallway where one is likely to brush against the rough wall surface and graze one's arms or knuckles.

Most extravagant of all textured papers are those made to look like reptile skin. For sheer glamour, exotic crocodile, snakeskin and lizard are hard to beat. Less adventurous tastes might settle for the soft allure of paper which looks like suede. In a similar way to suede cushions and upholstered furniture, suede walls will add warmth to a room and, at the same time, achieve a fashionable elegance. This is the look of covetable understatement which is, after all, what designers strive to achieve in a contemporary interior.

OPPOSITE *Anaglypta in a contemporary style gives a raised effect of coiled string to the surface of this squared design.*

RIGHT *Earthy colours and a rough open-weave finish give an ethnic texture to the walls.*

Raised texture

The revival of interest in natural materials in interiors has produced a whole host of woven-effect papers. The same method of production used to produce low-relief papers, known as anaglypta, which was developed in the 1870s, is used to manufacture many raised-effect papers today. The paper passes through a roller which has the design etched into the surface, so as it is put under pressure the paper is embossed with the three-dimensional surface decoration. It enables almost any style of design to be reproduced, whether contemporary or traditional. Both strong and practical, anaglypta papers are frequently used today in the same locations for which they were originally designed in the 1870s. As a dado, for example, anaglypta papers provide a tough and stylish surface which is extremely resistant to hard wear, so it is a practical choice for those areas of the home which are subject to a lot of wear and tear, like staircases and hallways. Anaglypta paper also provides a strong resistant surface for the walls of public spaces in hotels and stores.

Paper textures

The Japanese specialize in the production of papers made from natural materials. In addition to wood finishes they also make papers which incorporate fibres of grasses and seaweeds in their manufacture. These are undyed and look almost translucent, so the delicate strands of grass can be seen within the paper.

Handmade papers can incorporate little pieces of bark or tiny fragments of twigs, giving a more roughly textured, natural surface. All these natural papers have to be hung carefully as great care must be taken not to get paste on the surface. Once they are in place, however, these papers are naturally hardwearing.

New technology is enabling designers to experiment with innovative paper effects like pleating, folding and crushing, which have a handcrafted look, as if the paper has been laboriously applied to the wall. These crumpled textures seem to appear as a consequence of being scrunched up as they are applied, making a ridged, tactile surface. The result can be a random crackle effect or more formalized, when the creased lines of the paper are evenly measured across the wall. Either way the same striking tonal effects result, as the light is caught on one side of a crease while the other is sharply defined in shadow. More than with almost any other kind of wallpaper, the realization of the design depends on the source of light. A diffused light will seem to flatten the design, but in direct light the shadows from the lines will create sharp definition. These are papers whose textural impact is created almost as much by the planning of the lighting as by the actual design itself. The dynamics of the surface can be exploited by the interior decorator, and the way the design is applied to the wall will vary. Above all, it is a simple, effective way to create dramatic textures in contemporary interiors.

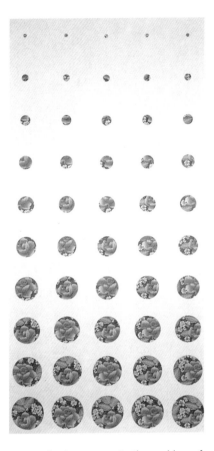

ABOVE *A witty answer to the problem of 'other people's wallpaper' is provided by this paper which is simply plain white with circular holes cut out at regular intervals along its surface. The idea is to paste it over the paper you inherit from the previous owners and make a positive design statement out of the last person's taste.*

LEFT *A formalized ridged design creates a checkered paper surface of balance and proportion.*

OPPOSITE *The random, three-dimensional folds of this innovative paper produce an intriguing surface texture.*

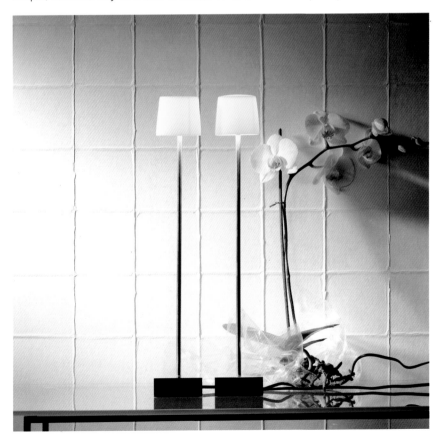

Wood-textured papers

There are many traditional wallpapers printed to imitate a wood finish, or to replicate the effect of tongue-and-groove boarding, or rustic Tyrolean panelling, or even elegant eighteenth-century French boiseries. The effect can be realistic, but papers which are made from real wood are striking in a different way.

Papers manufactured from real wood are made from the thinnest possible shavings, thinner even than the fine sheets used for wood inlay work. The shavings are applied in a regular pattern onto a backing paper so that they can be hung like conventional wallpaper. The designs vary according to how the strips have been laid down. Neat chevrons create a herringbone effect up and down the wall, while a simple square design acquires its interest and texture from the alternating direction of the wood grain. Intricate basketweaves have a three-dimensional effect as the wood appears to be woven across the wall, or thin vertical strips are differentiated from each other by variations in colour and tone.

The colours of the papers cover the natural shades of wood from pale blonde woods at one end of the spectrum, through warm honey tones to the dark cedars. Papers like these bring textural interest to the walls and envelop the whole room in warmth, a feeling created uniquely by natural materials.

Wood-textured papers are usually imported from Japan and they work particularly well with an Eastern style of decoration which relies on a few well-chosen pieces of furniture, lamps and rugs, carefully placed in the room to achieve a refined and uncluttered look. Antique pieces of furniture from the Far East are enhanced by this background, despite its contemporary look, although European antiques can seem uncomfortable. Yet contemporary European pieces which reflect the same natural simplicity can work together to produce an integrated design.

LEFT *The checkered texture of this wallpaper is made from the thinnest possible veneers of wood, cut into squares and pasted onto the background paper so that the grain runs in opposite directions, reflecting the light in different ways across the wall.*

OPPOSITE *A subtle wood-effect paper creates a relaxed air in this country-style setting. Wood panels run horizontally on the paper like a rustic interior in a simple timber house.*

Stone-textured papers

If the thought of a rough-textured wall surface that imitates the appearance of natural stone does not sound very appealing, then think again. Now is the time to reassess the merits of these tactile textured papers, as a host of high-quality stone-effect papers are currently being manufactured by leading design companies. Concrete and stone-effect papers are intended for large spaces, where the aim is to create an industrial look of pared-down economy, in an attempt to elicit the natural environment with the use of organic materials.

The beauty of these papers lies simply in the irregularity of the textured surface and the slightly glittery sparkle which is given off as the surface catches the light. While offering a neutral background for a domestic interior, stone-effect papers present a more interesting and natural-looking wall surface than plain painted walls.

Stone-effect papers are also useful for designers who want to create the minimal look of natural stone or concrete in a loft conversion, spacious store or restaurant where they cannot justify the cost of using the real material. Working with stone-imitation papers also solves all the practical problems of working with heavy blocks or sheets of natural stone. Once the wallpaper is in place it is hard to detect that the surface is not integral to the building.

LEFT *Old-fashioned garden roses are given fresh appeal by the introduction of a bright sky-blue background.*

OPPOSITE *A floral design inspired by archive material can still look fresh in a contemporary interior if accessorized in a simple way.*

Contemporary florals

The appeal of flowers is timeless and they have provided design inspiration for countless fabrics and wallpapers. Their desirability as a design motif lies in a combination of their soft colourings and the pleasing shapes into which flowers and leaves naturally fall. Add to this the lovely associations they bring to mind of summer gardens and lavish bowls of fresh flowers dotted about the house and you have the tranquil appeal of nature brought into your living space. Wallpapers may not be sweetly scented like the real thing, but they are equally uplifting. A flower-bedecked wallpaper looks pretty in a small country bedroom with a low ceiling and casement windows. Even in a small room it is possible to pile one floral design upon another in an uncontrived confection of patterns so that the wallpaper has a different design from the curtains, while cushions, bedspreads and rugs are different again. A complete floral theme such as this needs to be united by colour; otherwise it can become messy. A more sophisticated urban scheme is achieved if the floral wallpaper is set off against plain fabrics, or small, lightly woven designs like checks and spots, coordinating or contrasting with colours picked out from the flowers. An off-white background gives floral wallpapers a simple appeal so that even if they are faithful reproductions of antique designs the colour palette is fresh and modern.

Contemporary romantics

Romantic in contemporary wallpapers does not mean pretty in the conventional floral, sugary-pastel sense. It may mean instead voluptuous curves, softly feminine colours and designs with a strong linear quality of generous sensuality. Organic plant forms are the basis of many contemporary romantic designs. Free interpretations, rather than literal drawings of a botanical nature, give a fresh, innovative look to some of the most interesting wallpapers available today (see page 75), and designs which weave their way up the wall in freely moving fronds share this appeal (see page 83).

The colour palette is as important as the pattern. An ethereal feel is conjured up with light, fresh colours – the kind of colours which have a translucent clarity rather than a chalky matt appearance. While shades of cream, beige, taupe and vanilla are always popular in traditional interiors, a more singing palette of apple green, raspberry, lemon, lavender and rose will combine to create a light-enhancing and colourful interior, that is both romantic and pretty.

Designs of gentle swirling curves in subtle colours will fit into nearly any room and create a Zen-like feeling of peace and tranquillity. Many contemporary romantic papers appear to have an almost lyrical quality and in contrast to most repeat patterns seem to be hand-sketched across the wall like musical notation.

RIGHT *The period feel in these line drawings of nudes is reminiscent of the work of Eric Gill, a British painter and sculptor prominent in the 1930s. Arranged to create a patten on wallpaper, they impart an air of sensual delight and make a stylish and witty paper to hang in an intimate room such as a bathroom or bedroom.*

OPPOSITE *Sinuous curves flow across the wall in a design which takes its inspiration from the Art Nouveau style.*

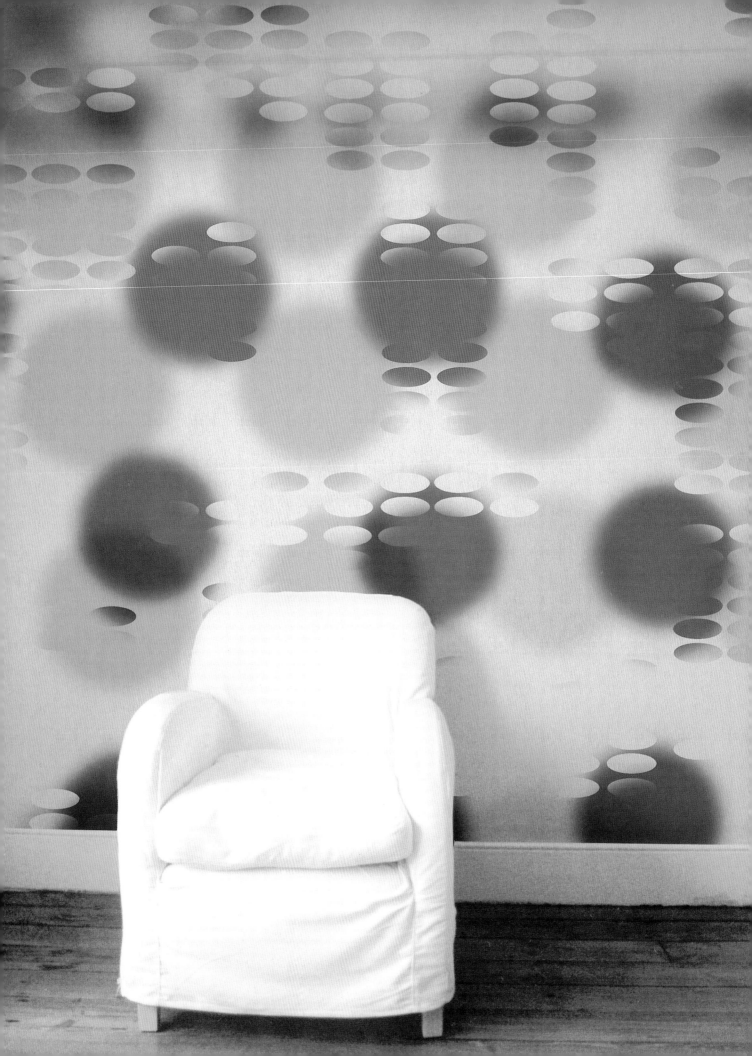

Computer-aided designs

With digital technology, wallpaper design has undergone a revolution. Computer-literate wallpaper designers now have the tools to experiment on a massive scale. They can now enlarge or stretch a pattern with the touch of a button to see how it will look if the design filled the entire length of the wall. A simple floral motif can be enlarged to such a point that it becomes almost abstract (see page 110), while photographic images can be manipulated on screen until they become unrecognizable versions of their former selves.

As a result, designers are at last free from the constraints of the wallpaper repeat – the single most inhibiting factor in wallpaper design for machine-made production. This inevitable repeat occurs every time the printing drum revolves, so the result is an image recurring every 60cm (24in) or so all the way up the paper.

Currently these new specialist printing techniques are an expensive option, and wallpaper made in this way is normally chosen for site-specific locations where the quality and impact of the design is a more important consideration than the price, and where a one-off wallpaper design is commissioned by enlightened

LEFT *This angular pattern was inspired by pages of a newspaper, but printed in shades of pale brown it has a simple, structured architectural quality which brings its own formality.*

OPPOSITE *Here, wallpaper design experiments with digital manipulation to produce an image in which the variations in focus appear to change the depth of perspective on the wall.*

clients in the same way as they might have commissioned a mural in the past. Digital technology has made the photographic image far more exciting as wall decoration than traditional paint techniques, and as the technology develops, the price will become less prohibitively expensive.

The challenge for the designer in manipulating an image on the screen is completely different from that of creating a conventional wallpaper design, which depends on the traditional skills of the artist in painting, drawing and interpretation. On a computer the imagination can be freed up by the technology itself and take off in wild directions. The skill lies in the originality of the idea and the ability to exploit it as a concept. It is this aspect of design – the importance of the total originality of the inspiration – which brings wallpaper design closer to art.

But modern technology has not replaced traditional techniques of wallpaper production. Far from it. Many of the most beautiful contemporary wallpapers are once again being handmade by silk-screen or using methods perfected before wallpaper production was mechanized. Like computer-aided design, these methods free up designers to work on a large scale with non-repeating images.

Yet, other designers moving between the disciplines of fashion design, graphic art and fabric printing have worked within the framework of mechanized wallpaper manufacture, helping to revive wallpaper designs in mass-production, keeping pace with the move in interiors towards a simpler decorative style.

ABOVE *Two different wallpaper designs were created by scanning plants in life-size onto a computer and then manipulating them to simplify their form and greatly increase their scale.*

OPPOSITE *A vivid photographic subject is reproduced as wallpaper by specialist digital printing techniques, which produce images throbbing with colour on a giant scale. This image is meant to be seen at 'wall size'.*

OPPOSITE *Tower-block housing provides an assertive urban image for this uncompromisingly modern paper. The artist uses her own paintings as inspiration for the wallpaper.*

RIGHT *A hugely overscaled design of a fork and spoon is screen-printed to fill an entire drop of wallpaper. These original designs are intended to be hung as single panels rather than as repeated images around the room.*

Original screen-printed papers

In addition to handprinting wallpaper, screen-printing techniques allow contemporary designers to produce small runs of beautiful papers with a repeat so large that it becomes almost unnoticeable. An entire image can fill a single drop of paper, so that wallpaper can be hung as independent panels instead of an endlessly repeating design around the room. Interestingly, the types of image that artists are experimenting with on a large scale include everyday household objects and high-rise buildings familiar in the urban environment. Like Warhol (see page 35) forty years before, this elevation of ordinary images makes us question what subject matter is worthy of display on our walls. Hung like this, wallpaper becomes more than mere surface decoration and begins to have the presence of a work of art. Seeing wallpaper as art seems to go against the grain but really there is little difference in producing a limited edition print, screen-printed by hand and hung on the wall, and producing a single panel design intended to be hung as a drop of wallpaper. The difference between art and wallpaper seems to have become blurred – the only problem that remains lies in convincing the world that wallpaper is not just limited to the mechanical process of repeat pattern-making. Perhaps wallpaper designers are too modest in their approach to their work and do not make such elevated claims for themselves.

decorative details

panels
Some wallpapers are designed to be hung as individual panels rather than as a continuous design around every wall of the room. Many contemporary wallpapers have such a strong simple image that a single panel – made up of one or two drops of paper – is enough to make a powerful design statement for the whole room. The panels of paper serves to create a focus of interest in one area of the room and give the wallpaper pattern contained within the panel the prominence of a framed painting or drawing on the wall.

ABOVE *This historic panel decoration is based on the style of designs which decorated rooms in ancient Rome. This eighteenth-century version was recreated on wallpaper by Jean-Baptiste Réveillon.*

OPPOSITE *An attractively simple design is given prominence by the white-painted border which frames it like a picture.*

Designing with panels

Not only do panels add a new aesthetic dimension to a room, they can alter its apparent physical dimensions. Interior designers know well that dividing a wall up into different sections can minimize problems of height and proportion. A dado with horizontal panels, for instance, will help lower a high ceiling. Similarly, a strong vertical panel arrangement will break up a long expanse of wall.

Panels can be made in whatever dimensions are necessary to achieve an arrangement that is pleasing to the eye. They may be of identical width, but to avoid a rigid uniformity reminiscent of a row of guardsmen, it is usually preferable to alternate wider panels with narrower ones. For a balanced look, make the space between and above them equal, even if the panels themselves are of different widths, but allow a slightly larger space between the bottom of the panel and the skirting (base) board or dado.

Panels impose certain constraints on the decorative scheme, simply because of the symmetry they introduce, bringing order to the walls and influencing the position of other decorative elements such as pictures, mirrors within the framework of the panel, and large pieces of furniture in front. But this should be regarded as a virtue rather than a problem because it helps reinforce the general feeling of balance, which is one of the most attractive aspects of panel decoration.

In large, high-ceilinged rooms, usually found in older houses, panels fit easily and naturally: some houses still have their original wood or plaster panelling, but if it has been removed, architectural borders can be used to simulate moulded panels that help restore the room's former elegance. Plain or patterned borders would work equally well, though they create quite a different effect. Smaller rooms with lower ceilings need carefully considered treatment, because panels might diminish their size. But there is no reason to be deterred, provided the decoration is kept simple and in proportion with the scale of the room.

Chinese wallpaper murals can also be hung as panels, because although they were planned and painted to be hung in an unfolding sequence around the wall, like a mural, each drop is complete in itself and can stand alone. Many eighteenth-century French Réveillon papers were also designed as panels and have accompanying borders which frame the panel like a picture. This same approach to panel decoration can be adopted for interiors today using suitable papers and coordinating borders to create an elegant formal style.

Not only walls but doors, screens and even ceilings can be effectively decorated with panels. Recessed panels in doors can be filled with the same paper as used on the walls. This can be particulary useful in a bedroom where a wall of fitted cupboards interrupts the decorative theme. In this situation, the wallpaper within the door panels should be trimmed to continue the rhythm of the

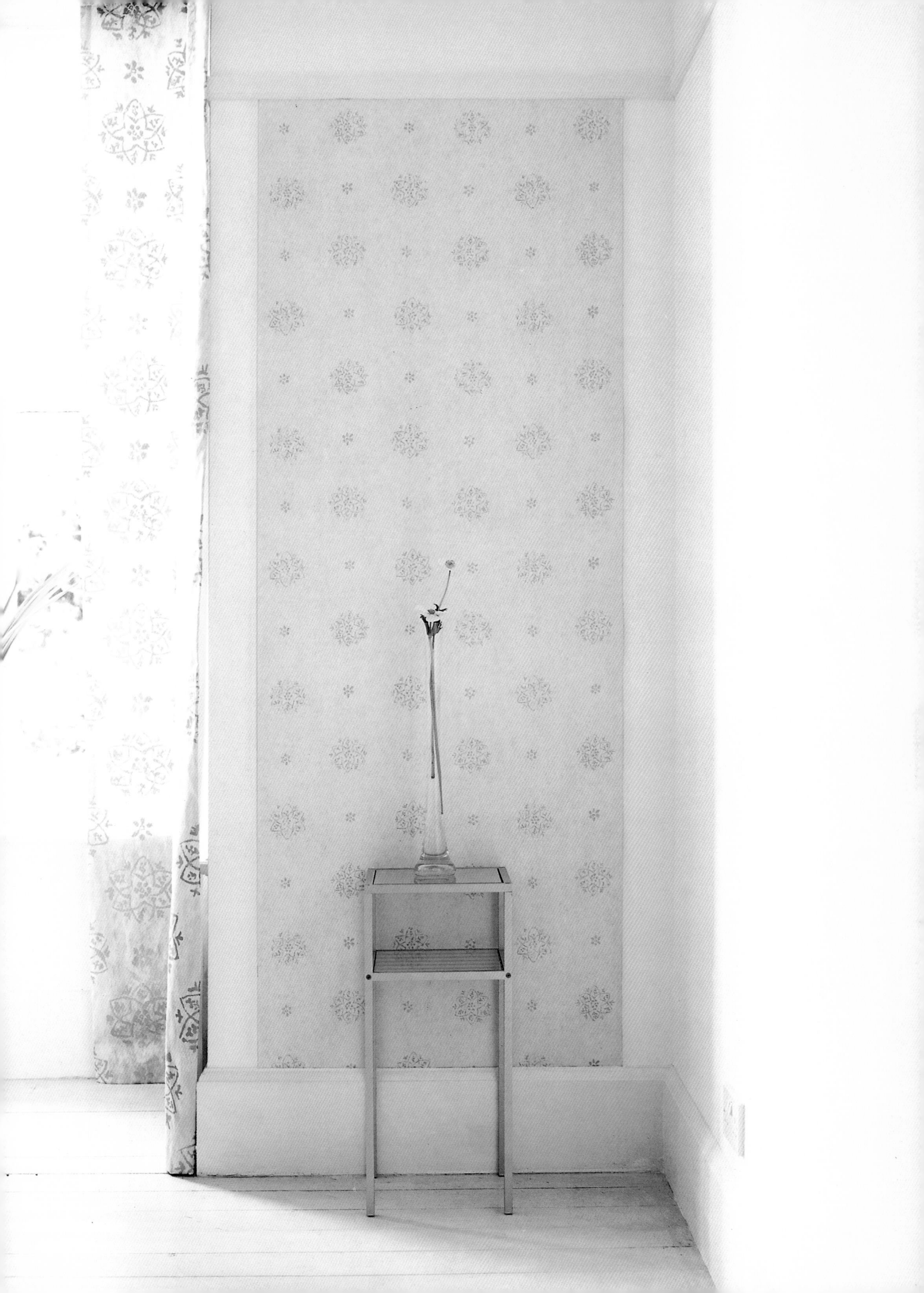

1. Chinese Decoration   2. Patterned Dado and Border with plain filling   3. Panelling effects by patterned borders on plain papers

pattern established on the other walls, but sometimes the style of the design may suggest an alternative arrangement. It is certainly best to avoid cutting straight through an important part of the pattern just for the benefit of symmetry. If the paper has a strong vertical element in the design, then it is especially important for balance to make this central within the panel.

Ceiling panels

The decoration of the ceiling is often neglected in contemporary fashion. In the past ceilings received just as much attention as walls – often even surpassing them in the extravagance of their embellishment. Today, however, most people simply paint them white or off-white and leave it at that. But in recreating an authentic period interior, consideration should be given to the decoration of the ceiling. If the ceilings are reasonably high, they can be decorated with panels of patterned paper, perhaps continuing or developing the theme of the walls. Some ceiling papers are manufactured especially for this purpose and look appropriate in period settings. The Edwardians, for example, used anaglypta to decorate the ceiling – its raised surface creating a three-dimensional design like plaster mouldings.

Border panels

The simplest panels are basically an extension of the border concept. If you paste a border all round the perimeter of a wall, you create, in effect, one large panel. By outlining further subdivisions of the wall, you can create a number of smaller panels, both vertical and horizontal. A discreet border simply defining a panel shape on a subtly patterned or textured paper contributes the same kind of understated elegance as both traditional wooden panelling or plasterwork.

Variations on this theme can be tried with papers of slightly different colours or tones within and outside the panels. If the same colour is used, a different finish inside the panel would also work well: a trompe l'oeil fabric-effect wallpaper, such as a damask or a silk moiré, or one with an interesting paint effect or stencil (see page 62), would add a new dimension and depth. These quite restrained approaches create a quiet and undemanding background for any interior. By contrast, papers and borders chosen for the richness of their pattern can be a great visual stimulus, inspiring the rest of the room decoration and creating a unique, personal style.

ABOVE *A variety of solutions to the perennial problem of how to cope with a long, narrow, featureless hallway are illustrated in* The Book of the Home, *published in England in 1925. As well as the introduction of pattern in the dado, panels are suggested as an effective and interesting means of breaking up the wall surface. Modern versions of these ideas, using up-to-date wallpapers, present different ways of hanging paper from the usual wall-to-wall, floor-to-ceiling approach.*

OPPOSITE *A beautifully handblocked 'Tree of Life' design is a traditional motif reinterpreted in muted colours which fits comfortably within panels of carved wooden mouldings on the side of a closet.*

Panels as frames

OPPOSITE *Wood grain wallpapers and borders achieve the effect of a panelled room. At the top a classical dentil frieze runs between wall and ceiling, while the dado and panels are made up from printed borders, designed to look three-dimensional. The carved flowers at the top of the panel echo the carving on the eighteenth-century chair below.*

BELOW LEFT *A wide geometric border panel provides further definition for the equestrian picture.*

BELOW RIGHT *Classical-style panels give a flat door a new look. The Roman head and urn were enlarged from smaller motifs and photocopied on brown paper to achieve an antique finish.*

If border panels are to contain pictures it is obviously important that the pictures are enhanced by the arrangement. There should be enough space around each picture for it to look balanced. If the picture frame overlaps the panel side it will seem awkward, so the size of the panels should be decided by the width of the chosen pictures.

Pictures often have much greater impact displayed in groups rather than being dispersed individually around the room. One panel containing perhaps two or three pictures, flanked by two empty panels, may look more effective than three panels each containing a single picture. Grouping pictures in panels offers an ideal opportunity to develop a specific visual theme. Important paintings make a statement in their own right, and clearly a good painting should hang on an appropriate background and be left at that. In the absence of a painting, a decorative statement can be made inexpensively by tapping into a variety of sources: a collection of inexpensive prints from a book, for example, might form a suitable image bank. They can be pasted directly to the wall in the manner of a print room (see pages 150–161).

Panels outlined with borders can equally well be used to display other decorative wall-hung objects. But choose the borders carefully: if they are too eye-catching they will detract from the impact of the central display.

Pompeiian hallway

The strong design images of ancient Pompeii are combined with colours that evoke the warmth of southern Italy. The decoration looks rich and rare, but it is not difficult to achieve. Two brushed paint-effect wallpapers in slightly different but harmonizing earth colours are used: the pinker-toned paper covers the walls, and the coral colour is used for the panels. The wide hand-printed border that frames the panels has a strong classical motif in black; this is balanced at the top of the wall and along the skirting (base) board by the bold interpretation of the Greek key pattern. A collection of classical prints is pasted directly to the wall. The designs are adapted from decorated vases found at Pompeii when it was first excavated in the eighteenth century, and the overall effect is reminiscent of Pompeiian wall paintings. Chairs with painted backs depicting similar motifs continue the classical theme. The black-painted table, however, is very much of the present and illustrates how well antique and contemporary styles can blend.

Panels of pattern

As well as creating the illusion of a panel by defining a space with a border, panels can be made specifically to contain and outline a particular wallpaper. There is an interesting historical precedent for this approach: in the eighteenth century wallpaper manufacturers such as Réveillon produced designs that were distinctive enough to be displayed in this way, as well as papers that were specifically intended to be hung as panels.

Certain wallpapers lend themselves beautifully to the panel treatment, and they can be used to transform or enliven a plain or simply-patterned background. Papers of contrasting colours, patterns and textures, papers that are simply too exotic, too rare or too expensive to be used in great quantities – all can look superb hung singly. By displaying a paper in a panel you draw attention to its special qualities. The intrinsic beauty of a hand-blocked design, for instance, can be enhanced by hanging it in a panel where its impact is not diluted by excessive repetition of the design motif.

If you choose an intensely patterned floral design, a small-scale repeat or a larger pattern that is complete over the width of one roll, the width of the panel will probably correspond with the width of the paper. In other papers, a major part of the design may fall on the edge of a roll, to be continued in the next drop. In this case a join can be made in the panel and the outside edges trimmed to the required width. A variety in panel width is not only more interesting, it allows you to select different parts of certain designs to make up the panels.

Choosing from a coordinated range put together by the manufacturer will ensure that borders and papers team successfully. Usually this is a range of plain or slightly textured wallpapers together with one that includes a pattern printed on top and a choice of borders to bring the theme together. This presents the opportunity to create an individual scheme to fit the room, with borders at ceiling and dado level, and different, but harmonizing, papers above and below. Many wallpaper companies include fabric for curtains and upholstery, designed to match or tone within the same collection, making the hard work of trying to match swatches become effortless. On the other hand, taking the whole scheme just as the designer intended can remove that spark of originality. No one should be afraid of putting something of themselves into these planned schemes.

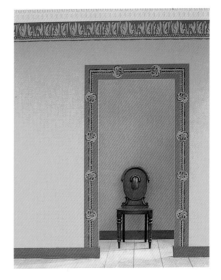

ABOVE *The borders frame the doorway and create a cornice below the ceiling, giving the room an architectural emphasis in design and colour.*

OPPOSITE *Timeless, classical design motifs from ancient Rome are reproduced on borders which are used to frame panels and prints to give an illusion of Pompeiian richness.*

Creating an illusion

There are, however, panel decorations which need to be purchased complete for them to make sense. The Ottoman tiled room, shown on this page, which so skilfully recreates the drama of blue-and-white ceramic tiles, would look distinctly odd if the sequence was interrupted. There are papers designed to look like books lining the walls of a library, which look convincingly effective if they cover all the walls of the room, like bookshelves, but can equally well be used just to cover the back of a door or a cupboard, or to make a single panel.

The simplest form of single panel decoration is created by using drops of wallpaper emphasized by plain borders. These paper borders can be cut from lengths of plain coloured paper or even painted directly onto the wall. Using single panels of paper is a way of making a more interesting decoration than simply dropping lengths of paper from ceiling to floor or wall to wall.

But you may wish to be more enterprising and mix papers and borders from different sources. In the absence of pattern, plain papers can be cut to virtually any shape you wish, enabling you to move beyond rectangular or square panels

OPPOSITE *Coordinating wallpapers and fabric are echoed by the panel hung behind the bed, outlined by three plain borders. The theme is emphasized by the placement of the pillows on layers of contrasting fabric.*

RIGHT *The exotic style of the Ottoman Empire is captured in a rich and intricate panel using different but complementary papers and borders. The designs are based on sixteenth-century Turkish tiles. Similar effects could be achieved using paisley borders and wallpapers, combining different designs to emphasize the Eastern influence in their beautifully complex patterns.*

and to introduce diamonds, triangles, circles, ovals and curves. The impact of the panel relies on the colour of the paper and the shapes created, and granite or marble or paint-effect papers are ideal for this kind of design treatment.

Restating the past

Some of the most challenging design ideas take their inspiration from the past, and the imitation marble panels in the eighteenth-century music room at Segerhof in Switzerland (below) provided the stimulus for this strikingly modern decoration (left). Marble panelling has a long pedigree – it was an important feature of classical interiors. The beauty of marble resides in the colours of the stone as well as in the shapes in which it is cut.

Natural stone finishes are popular today, and there are many faux marble papers available. Several different types – from extravagant hand-printed papers to inexpensive machine-made versions – are used in the panels on the left.

Designing a panelled room

It is sensible to begin working out a design like this on a small scale, cutting up pieces of paper to make a miniature version of the panel before committing yourself on a large scale. Experiment with their size and position on squared paper and then scale up the design to fit the intended location. The circle is used as a template for the semi-circular panel edges. This design is quite complex, but much simpler schemes can look equally effective. Plain marble papers in contrasting colours can be cut up into long, straight lengths to make simple borders around the room. This is a technique which works well if the plain border is cut to a reasonably generous width of 10–25cm (4–10in) and is pasted on the wall, up the corners, along the ceiling and above the skirting (base) board. It makes each wall into a panel of its own, defining and emphasizing the proportions of the room.

OPPOSITE *Panels cut from pieces of differently coloured marble belong to a long tradition of wall decoration. Here the concept has been adapted using several marble-effect wallpapers.*

LEFT *In this elegant nineteenth-century decoration, the classical model has been reinterpreted at Segerhof: marble wallpaper, printed in England, forms elegant panels, complete with decorative medallions of classical figures prominent on their black contrasting backgrounds.*

Pictorial panels

Beautiful hand-painted Chinese papers have traditionally been displayed in panels as well as in continuous panoramic decorations around the room, and in many historic houses it is still possible to see them hung in this way.

If the idea of a Chinese scenic paper appeals to you, and yet the thought of decorating an entire room seems overwhelming, panels provide the perfect solution. Importers of hand-printed Chinese designs at the luxury end of the market are usually prepared to sell just one set, of four to six panels, which can be hung together, split into smaller groups or hung individually around the room. If you anticipate moving house and taking these special panels with you, have them professionally mounted on wooden battens that can be removed from the wall.

While modern European and American wallpaper versions of Chinese designs are roller-printed and thus have repeating patterns, they can be treated in the same way, creating a pretty effect of Chinoiserie quite inexpensively. Arranged in twos or threes on a plain background, they introduce a delightful Oriental atmosphere. They may be hung like pictures or pasted to the wall and surrounded with paper borders; bamboo border designs would be a particularly apt choice.

Wonderful scenic panels, which exploited the exuberantly illusionistic techniques in which they excelled, were produced by French manufacturers at the beginning of the nineteenth century. Called décors, these were less ambitious

LEFT *Eighteenth-century Chinese papers, with characteristic hand-painted flowering branches, birds and foliage, grace this drawing room at Svindersvik in Sweden. Originally intended to run continuously as a panorama around the room, they have been hung here in separate panels with ornate gilt mirrors and windows in between the papered walls.*

BELOW *Chinese craftsmen still practise traditional painting skills and these four interlinking drops from a modern paper incorporate the most popular elements of antique designs.*

than panoramas, which filled the entire room, but were nonetheless far larger than any picture you would expect to find in a domestic setting. Hundreds of rich and vibrant colours were used in their production so that, even on close inspection, it is difficult to believe that they are not painted by hand. They depict scenes of lush vegetation and gardens full of flowers, or sometimes romantic landscapes or scenes from classical mythology. The viewer is transported into a world of illusion where a trompe l'oeil vista opens out from the room. Paper columns, pilasters, cornices, balusters, dados and friezes were used to frame the panels and suggested the edge of the room, while the landscape on the panel stretched out into the distance beyond. But eventually these architectural features assumed greater importance and became so decorative that the subject they framed could be left out and panels were created using just the pillars, dados and friezes.

Scenic panel decoration became popular again between the First and Second World Wars, when the subjects – usually landscapes – were printed in far fewer colours. This made them considerably less expensive and therefore more widely available than earlier decors.

Many people like the concept of scenic trompe l'oeil and would like to have a panorama in their home, but they are not always easy to track down. If you wish to pursue the idea, you may be able to obtain the elements you need to create a panorama from a specialist company; some produce modern versions of the pictorial garden scenes (see opposite) so popular in the past. Chinese panoramas similar in style to the eighteenth-century versions are still being painted in China today, and are available from specialist suppliers in Europe and the United States. Zuber, the oldest wallpaper company in the world (see page 23 and Directory pages 186-187) also still makes some of the original panoramas using some of the original block designs.

OPPOSITE *'Armida's Garden', one of the most celebrated of the extravagant French décor wallpaper panels, was awarded a medal at the 1855 Paris Exhibition. This large panel – a colourful and voluptuous expression of unruly horticultural delight – is the central part of a design incorporating smaller side panels. It measures 3.89 x 3.37m (12¾ x 11ft).*

BELOW *Hand-painted Chinese panels can be hung like this, in a continuous panorama, or in single drops to make individual decorative panels.*

borders, dados and friezes

The enormous range of wallpaper borders available today provides exciting opportunities for creating a different look – something far more individual in its impact than just plain walls or an uninterrupted expanse of wallpaper. Used in even the simplest, most restrained way, borders add an elegant and pleasing detail to an interior, as well as bringing a professional-looking finish. Used with imagination and panache, they have even greater potential for decorative innovation.

ABOVE *Many borders were originally designed to look like the gimp ribbon which was put at dado height to hide the pins securing fabric to the wall in the days before wallpaper was widespread. Here a selection of old designs have been revived in contemporary colours.*

OPPOSITE *The clean horizontal lines of the room are enhanced by the colour division on the wall, with a simple border in between.*

Borders have been used for almost as long as wallpapers themselves. Originally they were hung to conceal the tacks that held wallpapers in position, but by the late eighteenth century they had begun to assume real importance as a decorative feature in their own right. In addition to the many floral and decorative borders, which were very popular, a wide repertoire of architectural friezes and borders was produced. Many of these were printed to look like a cornice and hung at the junction of wall and ceiling to add grandeur to a room.

By the beginning of the nineteenth century designs had become extremely elaborate and superb trompe l'oeil swags and festoons, also for use at cornice level, were supplied with a straight border that could be used for outlining doors, windows and walls. French manufacturers in particular produced very luxurious and opulent swagged designs – heavily fringed and tasselled velvets, festoons of silk caught in knots and adorned with flowers, foliage, ribbons and feathers.

By the end of the nineteenth century, when it became fashionable to divide walls into three bold horizontal areas, each with a different patterned paper, in the dado-filler-frieze formula (see page 142), borders were often used between them, providing the opportunity to introduce yet another pattern. This very intensely patterned decoration was gradually superseded by a simpler style in which the frieze became deeper and more dominant, often surmounting a discreet paper or just a tall wooden dado.

Twentieth-century revivals of interest have produced some imaginative approaches to borders, notably in the 1920s and 1930s when an immense variety of styles and colours were both inexpensive and readily available. Borders with the edges cut to follow the intricacies of the design along one side were widely used. Motifs of fruit, flowers and foliage, often outlined in black and vibrantly coloured, made a strong decorative impact and were much in demand for the enlivening effect they had on cheap and undistinguished papers.

Some of the most useful borders available today enable you to add architectural detailing, such as a ceiling cornice to a bare room. Inexpensive contemporary border designs, some created with reprints of archive designs, are also available from wallpaper manufacturers, and many have coordinating wallpapers, with which to create interesting and attractive effects. Indeed this is an area of interior design where bold imaginative treatment can more than make up for a small budget.

There are innumerable collections of wallpaper produced with their own borders which will create a coordinated look that is simple to devise and gives an attractive decorative scheme which you can visualize easily from the picture in the wallpaper sample book. With imagination, a more individual result can be achieved by combining borders and wallpapers which were not designed with this in mind, perhaps even from different manufacturers.

With a boldly designed border, a plain textured paper with a discreet pattern motif will often provide the best background because it allows the design on the border to take a more prominent part in the overall interior scheme.

Borders as dados

Using a border as a dado will create a strong horizontal division in the room, especially if the colour of the wallpaper above and below the dado is different. This will seem to have an effect on the proportions of the room as well as its style. A dark colour below the dado will bring weight to the bottom of the wall and give substance to the decoration. Doing it the other way round and hanging a lighter colour at the bottom and the darker one above may look awkward and will not anchor the decorative scheme visually.

RIGHT *A delicate flower-patterned wallpaper is enhanced by a matching border, where the motif is more densely printed.*

OPPOSITE *A striking interior decoration scheme uses black for maximum impact. The black dado paper anchors the honey yellow scheme and the two are linked by a striking border which combines elements of both papers.*

RIGHT *A delicate hand-painted leaf-and-flower border is used lavishly to define each wall in this bedroom at Drottningholm, a restored eighteenth century castle not far from Stockholm, Sweden.*

Defining space and enhancing proportion

Borders are the simplest and most versatile means of defining space and uniting design elements and are most effective if they are planned as an integral part of the decorative scheme. The simple addition of a border around the top of a plain painted or papered wall can transform a room; not only does it give emphasis and character to the wall, it draws the eye upwards, providing a balance with other elements – furniture, carpets, ornaments – which claim the attention at a lower level.

Borders are extremely useful for enhancing, or altering, the proportions of a room. A high ceiling can be lowered visually by the addition of a paper border at dado-rail level. This also provides the opportunity of introducing a different patterned paper beneath, either for practical reasons – in which case it might be tougher, darker and more highly patterned than the paper above, in order not to show marks – or just for the visual pleasure of an agreeable combination of papers. Continuing the idea up the stairs in a hallway will add interest to an otherwise featureless expanse of wall.

A wide border or frieze pasted along the wall at picture-rail level will also reduce the apparent height of a room, particularly if the ceiling colour is continued down to the level of the border and a contrasting paper is hung beneath it. The same lowering effect is achieved by a wide border pasted next to the ceiling as a cornice. If it is not possible to find a wide border to match a scheme, a combination of two or three widths of the same border will add the required weight and balance. Although in principle you should not be deterred from using a wide border simply because a room is small – hung imaginatively it could make an exciting decorative contribution – if the ceiling is very low, a wide border at the top of the wall would make it appear lower still.

Awkward or odd angles – a sloping attic ceiling, for example – can be turned to good advantage with borders outlining the angles to emphasize their quirky character. But beware of drawing attention to features that might be better underplayed, such as windows of different heights and sizes, an off-centre mantelpiece, or an uneven ceiling in an old house. For problems such as these, rather than using borders, choose a form of decoration that will make them less noticeable: a busy floral pattern can cover a multitude of sins.

In rooms of elegant proportions one of the most pleasing treatments of all is to use the border like a picture frame, outlining the wall at its edges and drawing attention to the wall itself as a distinct unit that makes an attractive background against which to display furniture and pictures. A more flamboyant approach might take its cues from the past, using attractive borders to draw attention to the room's architectural detailing by outlining doors, windows and fireplace.

As well as looking attractive, borders help to hide the tiny mistakes in paper cutting which often spoil the work of an inexperienced paperhanger and enable you to create a professional-looking finish. (Practical instructions for hanging borders, dados and friezes are given on pages 178-181.)

Designing with borders

The easiest way to choose borders and wallpapers which look good together is to consult the manufacturers' pattern books, where coordinating borders are shown as variants on the design of the main wallpaper. The general intention is to take a single design idea and rework it in a variety of different ways. There are pretty florals to team with delicate sprigged papers, and richly ornamented patterns which develop the theme of the accompanying wallpapers. Plain or very discreetly patterned papers are presented with striking borders that give the paper more impact. Archive designs are reproduced in both their original versions and in modern colours. These papers and borders are all carefully matched to work together, giving the chance to create visual variety and the confidence to know that whatever combinations you choose will look attractive.

When coordinating border designs are printed on the same background as the matching wallpaper, the join between the two is invisible once they are on the wall. Thus quite complicated design images may seem to flow freely around the top of the wall, just as if they were an integral part of the main wallpaper.

Coordinating borders and papers are easy to use but there is no need to follow the manufacturers' suggestion. Many original – and often far more interesting – combinations can be put together using borders from one source and papers from another.

BELOW *A bold neo-classical border provides an appropriately important finish to an unusually striking wallpaper.*

Architectural borders

These architectural borders are designed to look like the kind of moulded plaster decoration that is commonly used to finish rooms in all but the most contemporary domestic interiors.

But detailing of this kind is often left out in modern houses and may often have been removed in older houses the last time it was fashionable to take everything back to unadorned walls. It is possible, but very expensive, to replace plaster mouldings or to introduce them where none have existed. Fortunately, however, architectural borders are produced by many wallpaper manufacturers, and they offer an effective substitute. They are usually based on the classical repertoire of design motifs, freely interpreted in different sizes from simple narrow beading to the wider egg-and-dart patterns and large scroll and acanthus leaf designs. They are often printed in trompe l'oeil so that the paper gives the effect of standing out proudly from the wall.

Architectural borders are most effective in natural colours: grisaille, cream, terracotta. Where moulded decoration already exists on the ceiling, an architectural border can be positioned at the top of the wall to continue the theme. They are visually unobtrusive while at the same time contributing significantly to the character of the room. A simple egg-and-dart motif in a small room looks appropriate. In a room with higher ceilings, you can be more adventurous, with a wider cornice design. While architectural borders are clearly not a suitable choice for rooms with very low ceilings, they can enhance the plain walls of modern houses bringing an architectural finish which did not exist before.

RIGHT *Borders with classical inspiration range from Greek key, scroll, palmette and arabesque designs.*

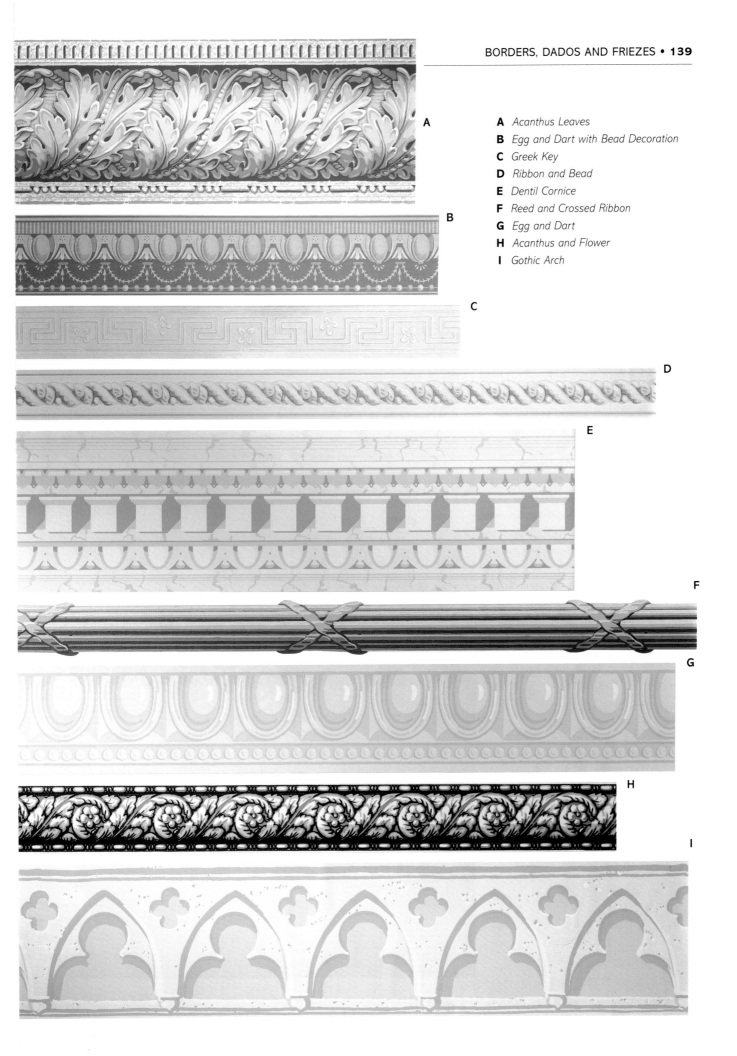

A *Acanthus Leaves*
B *Egg and Dart with Bead Decoration*
C *Greek Key*
D *Ribbon and Bead*
E *Dentil Cornice*
F *Reed and Crossed Ribbon*
G *Egg and Dart*
H *Acanthus and Flower*
I *Gothic Arch*

Historical dados and friezes

A dado is a traditional method of dividing the wall space into separate areas and enhancing its proportions. Usually rising from the skirting (base) board to about chair-back height, it divides the wall horizontally and serves both a decorative and a functional purpose. As an architectural device for adding refinement to a blank wall it may be represented simply by a wooden or plaster rail marking the division or, more importantly, it can be an entire panelled section.

Wallpapers produced as dados were originally copies of panelling, designed to bring an inexpensive practicality to a room. Some were fairly plain, others might be filled with elaborate decorative rosettes and medallions. The dado papers were designed to be used in conjunction with panoramic papers, which were so popular at the beginning of the nineteenth century, and often represented suitably imposing balustrades that established the architectural boundary for the scene beyond.

Dados were often designed with matching 'friezes', most of which, until the late nineteenth century, were basically rather wide and elaborate borders: the majority were architectural in inspiration, though swags of flowers and draperies were also popular. Today a frieze usually implies a significantly wider border of the kind that assumed great importance in the final decade of the nineteenth century.

In the 1870s and 1880s the Victorians, not noted for their restraint in matters of decoration, took every opportunity to indulge the fashionable taste for rich pattern. It was thought dull in the extreme to use one wallpaper only and preferable by far to introduce at least two other patterned papers – as dados and friezes – to sandwich a central expanse of filler paper. The proportions varied according to whim; dados, for example, were often taken considerably farther up than chair-back height, and friezes could be as deep as 1.2m (4ft), leaving a very narrow filler. Thus a great variety of decorative schemes was achieved, though such intense combinations of pattern on the wall tended to make rooms appear smaller and less formal. Sometimes the same papers – or even different ones – were repeated on the ceiling, creating a rich, dense, intricate effect which to modern tastes seems overpowering to say the least.

A more restrained version of the idea using different papers and borders can certainly look attractive today, but it is important to choose papers that complement each other in design and colour. A patterned dado, a plain paper above and two harmonizing borders – one at the top of the dado, one at the top of the wall – can produce an interesting combination, and some pattern books show wallpapers and borders already selected to work in this way. A plain dado with a pattern above is a more conventional combination, which can be enlivened with a striking border. Stripes, too, work well in this context, especially in halls and stairways when they are combined with a plain paper.

Contemporary dados

If you want to recreate an authentic nineteenth-century-style dado there are many suitable designs to choose from. If the main purpose of the dado is practical – to withstand the wear and tear likely in a hallway, for example – then the sturdy Lincrusta, a linoleum-based material, or anaglypta, a cotton paper, both very widely used in Victorian times, are still available (see page 94). Both Lincrusta and anaglypta have a raised, patterned surface tough enough to stand up to most bumps and scratches.

OPPOSITE *As many as six or seven different patterns might be piled one on top of the other in the Victorian dado-filler-frieze combination. Though such mixtures of design and colour are unlikely to appeal today, a judicious selection of harmonizing papers makes for a lively and interesting decoration.*

RIGHT *The hallway in this Edwardian house is decorated in authentic period style. A reproduction Lincrusta as a dado, heavily embossed with a characteristic stylized flower design, is painted the same green as the oak leaves on the William Morris wallpaper.*

OPPOSITE *Wallpapers inspired by original nineteenth-century designs are used in this restoration of a Victorian mansion in Melbourne, Australia. The base of the decoration is the dado, a heavily patterned paper covering the lower part of the wall. A border divides it from the filler paper above – a simple design of repeating Greek palm-leaf pattern printed in gold on a pale celadon background. The theme is picked up on a larger scale in the wide frieze at the top of the wall.*

By the last decade of the nineteenth century, the fashion for the multiple arrangement of the dado-filler-frieze started to wane. People began to prefer a simpler style of decoration in which the dado was virtually abandoned, while the frieze went from strength to strength. A discreetly patterned paper would be hung from floor to picture rail and above it was pasted a wide, boldly designed, brightly coloured frieze – the focal point of the decoration. As the fashion for friezes spread, many different and highly distinctive designs became available. Decorators could choose between the panoramic impact of a romantic landscape unfolding around the top of the room or a repeating pattern of flowers and foliage in the Art Nouveau manner perfected by the eminent wallpaper designer William Shand Kydd. While Shand Kydd's stencilled and hand-blocked designs represented the height of achievement in art wallpapers of the day, many other more prosaic frieze subjects were also available. Sporting motifs, nursery characters and storybook scenes were enormously popular, and there was scarcely a room in the house for which an appropriate frieze could not be found.

Such popularity was bound, eventually, to produce counter-reaction, particularly among those with pretensions to taste. By the end of the first quarter of the twentieth century, manufacturers began to encourage this counter-reaction by supplying all the elements needed to make different arrangements on the walls: cut-out motifs, borders and cornerpieces that could be combined to create decorative panels.

Today only a few wallpaper companies supply wide friezes, which are either reprints of original designs or fresh interpretations of the traditional idea. However, if the type of frieze you want is not commercially available, it is always possible to improvise and create your own. One very simple way to get the effect of a strong decorative band at the top of the wall is to use the entire width of a wallpaper which works equally well hung horizontally as vertically.

wall decorations
When walking around the older parts of any large city your attention is likely to be focused on the many distractions at street level. Yet a glance upwards may be richly rewarded, for on buildings more than fifty years old, it is likely to reveal an astonishing wealth of decorative architectural detail. Buildings without such embellishment are a twentieth-century phenomenon and many of them are now widely disliked because they present such a plain face to the world.

ABOVE *Trompe l'oeil wall decorations can be used to create the illusion of mouldings. Some of these paper ornaments are presented already cut out, so they can be combined in many different ways.*

OPPOSITE *Trompe l'oeil wall trophies representing art and music set the theme for an elegantly classical room in the eighteenth-century manner. Pasted to a plain wallpaper background, these cut-out elements stand out clearly like the plasterwork which inspired them.*

Highly ornamented façades were once commonplace in both public and domestic architecture, and were by no means confined to grand buildings. By the end of the nineteenth century decorative devices in stone or plaster were being mass-produced and builders could order the elements they wanted from catalogues crammed with a vast range of ready-made architectural ornament. Thus the doors and windows of even quite modest houses came to be flanked by classical pillars and topped by a fine cornice or triangular pediment, while additional embellishment might be introduced by stylized flower garlands, wreaths, flowing ribbons and bows. This was a continuation of a tradition that favoured an elegant finish as a way of bringing character and style to a building.

Decorative plasterwork

Such ornamentation was, of course, as important a feature of interiors as it was of exteriors. At its simplest, decorative plasterwork was used to describe the structure of the room, in the form of moulded borders or friezes. In grander houses, however, it was used to decorate the wall surface with large and elaborate motifs often taken from classical sources. In eighteenth-century England this sort of decoration ranged from the formalized panels, trophies and friezes in the style of Robert Adam to the exuberant swirls and asymmetry of the Rococo, with its strong Chinese influence. Even more opulent decoration can still be seen in stately homes and palaces whose walls and ceilings are decorated with complex and lavish scenes incorporating three-dimensional figures. The motifs were not always classical, however, and the Victorians also turned to medieval styles for decorative inspiration: Gothic ornament is characteristic of the second half of the nineteenth century in both interior and exterior decoration.

In houses that did not have this three-dimensional decoration, similar effects could be achieved with paper ornaments printed as highly convincing trompe l'oeil pastiches of moulded plasterwork and carved wood. They, too, were available in a wide variety of designs and decorators could create their own arrangements from collections of motifs which were supplied in sheet form ready to be cut out and pasted to walls and ceilings.

Later, different styles of paper ornament evolved. Cornerpieces for panels, little pictorial vignettes, and oval medallions in decorative cartouches and geometric shapes were produced to add interest to otherwise plain walls. Elaborate borders with an intricate cut-out bottom edge were combined with these elements. They were fun to use and brought a pleasurable degree of individuality to the decoration. Some of the same kind of elements are available today from specialist companies and give the opportunity for recreating this elaborate style of plasterwork wall decoration.

Among the elements available to purchase are the trompe l'oeil decorations, illustrated here and on page 147, which take their inspiration from architectural themes and from the kind of decorative motifs that in the past were rendered in stone, stucco, plaster or wood.

Wall decorations

This is a romantic style of wall decoration which plays on the idea of trompe l'oeil illusion to create interesting effects. Wall decorations are a clever way of introducing a period feel to a room which is otherwise completely plain and devoid of mouldings, cornice or any other embellishment. Thus a simple room can be transformed by the addition of decorations which look like elaborate plasterwork. Most of these wall decorations are classical in style and take their themes and motifs from eighteenth-century mouldings, but there are also collections in the Gothic style which give a different effect – either light and delicate pointed arches and quatrefoils in the manner of eighteenth-century Gothick, popularized by Horace Walpole, or in a more robust nineteenth-century Gothic style. It gives the opportunity to create an individual decoration.

ABOVE *The ceiling of a tiny square bathroom is enlivened by trompe l'oeil cut-out decorations. Flying cherubs, linked with garlands and bows and pasted against a blue-grey paper, appear to cavort about the sky.*

RIGHT *The three-dimensional appearance of these friezes and borders creates the effect of intricate plaster moulding. Even such small amounts of plaster detailing can set the style for the entire room, and the pointed arches, quatrefoils and rosettes here combine to achieve a delightful echo of eighteenth-century Gothick style.*

Using paper ornaments

Paper ornaments are supplied already cut out and are intended to be used in a variety of ways. You can either set the theme for a room, using a range of elements to achieve the effect and creating architectural elements like panels, borders and friezes, or you can use a few pieces to decorate mantelpieces, alcoves and recesses, or indeed any area which you want to make a focal point. If you begin working with paper cut-out decorations on a small scale and are pleased with the result, this may give you the confidence to attempt a more ambitious setting later.

Because paper ornaments are supplied as individual pieces it is possible to create an arrangement which works, whatever the proportions of the room. Pieces can be linked together to form a continuous border, by increasing or decreasing the gaps between decorative elements to exactly fit your room's dimensions.

BELOW *Garlands of fruit and flowers linked with rosettes form a swagged border beneath the cornice in this drawing room. The arrangement over the fireplace finishes with two drops in a similar style, creating a focal point on the mantelpiece. The area is further embellished with bows and ribbons from which the small oval portraits appear to be suspended.*

print rooms

One of the more whimsical decorative inventions of the eighteenth century was the creation of a print room. Formal reception rooms were covered from dado to cornice with a collection of prints, not conventionally framed and hung but cut out in a variety of shapes – circles, octagons, ovals, rectangles – and then pasted directly onto the wall. Printed cut-out paper borders pasted around individual prints gave the illusion of frames and helped to create the illusion of a picture gallery.

ABOVE *The elements required for the creation of a print room are supplied by specialist companies printed on large sheets of paper.*

OPPOSITE *Lady Louisa Connolly created one of the prettiest eighteenth-century print rooms at Castletown in Ireland. She cut the prints in a variety of shapes – octagons, ovals, circles, squares – and arranged them in distinct groups, using printed paper embellishments to create a highly decorative arrangement. Garlands and bows crown the larger groups, while swags and ribbons link the pictures below. Within the groups there is a great degree of symmetry, with pairs of smaller prints balancing larger ones. Grouping prints – rather than pasting them in a more random fashion over the entire wall area – is an approach that can be successfully adopted today.*

The overall effect of pasting prints to the wall was of a crowded but elegant picture gallery, with the formality enlivened by the addition of cut-out paper swags, garlands of flowers, printed ribbons and classical ornaments pasted around the prints to link groups and create a decoratively pleasing composition.

Making a print room is an enjoyable way of creating a very personal decoration, and this, no doubt, is one of the reasons why the fashion was originally adopted with such enthusiasm. Nor is it difficult to do, whether you choose to decorate in authentic eighteenth-century style or decide on a more up-to-date interpretation of the idea.

While early print rooms would have been hung with black-and-white engravings or mezzotints, an authentic look can be achieved today with reproductions, though it is still possible to come across inexpensive original prints. But do not be afraid to cheat a little if you wish: good photocopies can be given the patina of age by the use of cold tea, and will look quite convincing once in place. The choice of subject matter is virtually limitless. Apart from the traditional Old Master subjects, landscapes and architectural vistas, there are portraits of the famous and infamous, kings and courtiers, actors and musicians, and prints depicting every possible subject from ballooning to botany, from marine life to high fashion.

A single subject or theme can provide the inspiration for an entire room. Alternatively a disparate collection of prints will bring variety and interest. Obvious places in which to search are shops specializing in the sale of old prints, but antique shops and stalls are also a good source. An entire collection of similar prints could be taken from an existing book. Though you might be reluctant to break up an old book for this purpose, many old prints will in fact have been derived from this source. The most unlikely place may yield an exciting discovery and a few more prints to add to a growing collection.

In the eighteenth century, black-and-white engravings were cheap and plentiful, and if colour was required it was often painted in by hand. Many of the antique engravings found today have been coloured in this way only recently and, to the purist eye, have been spoilt. But if you are not attempting historical authenticity it is effective to adapt the idea to a more modern idiom and use contemporary coloured prints.

Choosing images

Colour prints are inexpensive, so it is simplicity itself to make a collection of pictures, posters, or prints in colour to create a modern interpretation of the print room. It is important, however, to choose prints which harmonize in both colour and style. A selection of botanical prints taken from a calendar, for example, can

ABOVE *Even bathrooms can be given the print room treatment. The size and subject matter of these large prints – photocopies of Piranesi engravings – call for wide, bold frames and cornerpieces. Their impressive formality is agreeably counterbalanced by walls painted a sunny dandelion yellow.*

RIGHT *A print room decoration on an unusually strong background colour transforms this hall into a bright and welcoming space. The archway, its most arresting feature, is enhanced by the circular prints hung to echo its shape.*

provide the basis of a delightful decoration. Prints such as these may often be enhanced by a variety of different wallpaper borders chosen to complement the scheme of the room. You can make even simpler borders by mounting the prints on coloured paper.

Large prints can be framed effectively using conventional wallpaper borders but the borders should be cut to finer widths, if necessary, so as not to overwhelm smaller ones. Cutting modern prints in a variety of interesting shapes, in the traditional manner, will help create a lively composition. Those that have a white background can easily be cut into circles, octagons or diamonds without spoiling or encroaching on the subject matter. Experimenting like this can be great fun, and you will achieve an unusual form of decoration and a very personal interpretation of the print room concept.

As in the past, the idea can be exploited virtually anywhere in the house, though it is particularly effective in small rooms. Using picture imagery is also an attractive way of decorating a hall or staircase, imaginatively replacing those framed pictures that can so easily be damaged in such confined spaces. Use cut-out paper decorations to link the prints in pairs or groups to create a more unified impression. This is also an idea worth adopting for a child's playroom. Postcards, prints, birthday cards and reproductions of children's book illustrations can all provide material that is pleasing to arrange, and a source of delight for children.

Eighteenth-century print rooms

Collecting prints is – and was – part of the pleasure. In the eighteenth century many were acquired on the Grand Tour – a cultural tour of the major cities of Europe, particularly Italy – undertaken by young gentlemen and others of independent means who wanted to extend their classical education. Just as the modern tourist returns with postcards and colour prints as reminders of the original paintings seen in the Prado in Madrid or the Louvre in Paris, so no visit to Florence or Rome was considered complete without the purchase of several architectural prints of classical ruins or of Renaissance works of art.

At the same time printmakers in London and Dublin were reproducing many

ABOVE *Botanical prints form the basis of this collection. They have been skilfully hung as a uniform group along the top, with a balanced arrangement of different shapes and sizes beneath. A narrow print border edges the walls and emphasizes the pretty arched window frame.*

different kinds of paintings in print form, so there was considerable choice without venturing overseas. These black-and-white engravings covered an enormous range of subjects. As well as reproductions of Old Masters, classical and mythological scenes and architectural views, there were many different types of statues, busts and urns readily available and inexpensive enough to be cut up and pasted permanently to the wall. Responding to demand, the same printers also produced specially designed sheets of borders and decorative devices, which were used to embellish the prints.

The inspiration for the print room is thought to have come from Italy, where scholars and noblemen would sometimes have the top of a wall decorated with a frieze of black-and-white etchings, interspersed with small bronze statues. It was Lord Cardigan who was credited with introducing the idea to England. From his collection of fine prints he selected enough to cover the walls of a small room and framed them with specially printed borders. This was the room that inspired Horace Walpole, an eighteenth-century writer and connoisseur with a passion for decorative innovation, to create a print room at his home at Strawberry Hill, outside London. He described it in a letter to a friend as 'a bedchamber, hung with yellow paper and prints, framed in a new manner invented by Lord Cardigan, that is, with black and white borders printed'.

Print room creators

The vogue for creating print rooms was to last for more than seventy years, but it seems to have been principally confined to England and Ireland. That the fashion may have crossed the Atlantic to New England is suggested by an advertisement, dated 1784, proclaiming that one Joseph Dickinson of Philadelphia was available to 'superintend or to do the business of hanging rooms, colouring ditto plain or with any device of prints, pictures or ornaments, to suit the taste of his employers'. But no print rooms survive in North America.

Some print rooms were created by professionals, others were made by the houseowners themselves and can still be seen in their original setting. One of the oldest surviving rooms is at Castletown, a large classical house in Ireland (see page 151). It is thought to be the work of Lady Louisa Connolly, who arrived there as a young bride at the age of fifteen. She clearly found great pleasure and occupation in the decoration of the house and – since it was usual for aristocratic ladies of the time to become accomplished in the decorative arts – it was natural that she should have undertaken the print room project herself. Lady Louisa was obviously not very interested in architectural ruins and almost all the prints are figure compositions reproduced from Old Master paintings. Several of the portrait subjects are surrounded by pretty oval and circular frames and the prints are arranged in groups linked with garlands of flowers and printed ribbons. Interspersed among the prints are intricate trophies of dead game, possibly a reference to the sporting pursuits of the family. Though the painted wall on which the prints are mounted has now aged to a rather muted cream, it retains a freshness which enhances the prints and ornaments.

Thomas Chippendale, far more widely known for his cabinet-making than his association with paper hanging, is thought to have created more than one print room. An itemized bill for work carried out in 1762 at The Hatch, a country home in Ashford, Kent, certainly shows his involvement in this kind of decoration. As well as charging for materials, inter alia, '180 ft of Papie Mashie Border Painted

ABOVE *A luxurious hand-printed wallpaper designed in 1990. The separate elements could be cut out to suit your decoration.*

OPPOSITE *Making a print screen allows you to experiment with ideas on a smaller scale. In this handsome example, a rich velvety red makes a vibrant background to an imposing group of prints. Screens can serve a practical purpose in keeping out draughts or hiding things you do not wish to see, as well as being decorative.*

ABOVE *A circular print of the Wellington shield is the focal point in a print room at Stratfield Saye made by the Duke of Wellington himself. It introduces variety to an otherwise strictly ordered and formal arrangement.*

OPPOSITE *A clever trompe l'oeil wallpaper which appears to be a collection of antique business cards pasted on to a background paper. It has the effect of an unusual print room.*

Blue and White, 506 Printed Borders, 103 festoons, 74 Knots, 28 baskets and 8 Sheets of Chains,' Chippendale charged for labour. By far the largest part of the bill, as may be imagined, was for 'Cutting out the Prints, Borders and Ornaments and Hanging them in the room complete.'

Though prints were traditionally pasted on a neutral-coloured background, it was decided to paint the walls blue in the restoration of the print room at Ston Easton Park near Bath in Somerset. Like many other print rooms originally created in the eighteenth century, this one had suffered over the years from the effects of damp. Fortunately, old photographs were available showing the room in better times, and these were used as a guide when the room was restored in the 1960s. Ston Easton is a perfect example of the delicacy of early print rooms.

While a highly ornamented, decorative look characterized the early print rooms, by the beginning of the nineteenth century the general impression was far more restrained and austere.

The Duke of Wellington, on his return to England in 1815 and fresh from his victory over Napoleon at Waterloo, was presented by the British government with a large sum of money to purchase a country estate. He chose Stratfield Saye in Hampshire, previously owned by Lord Rivers, who had created a magnificent print room in the gallery using Shakespearian characters as his subjects. The room inspired the Iron Duke to make several print rooms of his own in the bedrooms and in a small sitting room. It is not surprising that the latter had a military theme: uniformed soldiers, battle scenes, the Duke himself, and even a print of his old foe Napoleon filled the walls. There are no delicate chains, garlands or ornamental devices to add lightness to the design: the scheme is rigidly symmetrical, a very different though nonetheless interesting interpretation of the print room concept.

Modern revivals

Gradually the enthusiasm for print rooms began to wane, and it was no longer fashionable to decorate an entire room in this way. Few original print rooms have withstood the passage of time, and there are only about fifteen still in existence. However, over the last thirty years there has been a growing interest in their restoration. When the National Trust decided to recreate the flood-damaged print room at Blickling Hall in Norfolk, they made careful copies of all the original bows and borders as they were removed from the walls.

It is possible to commission a complete print room made especially for you by specialists in this field or, if you are inspired to make your own and have plenty of time and enthusiasm to undertake all the necessary paper cutting and trimming, then it is possible to purchase the sheets from Ornamenta Ltd and Nicola Wingate-Saul (see pages 186–187). Both these suppliers have put together complete sets of sheets for making a print room together with detailed instructions and advice to help you get started. All that needs to be done is to begin with a collection of your own prints which need framing. The best advice is not to be too ambitious at first, but to keep the design small and manageable.

The idea of the print room has also been interpreted in wallpaper, which makes it possible to achieve the effect without all the time-consuming labour. Of course the design is not totally unique, but many people would prefer that to the prospect of spending hours cutting up tiny pieces of paper.

RIGHT *A set of print room sheets together with a few prints are all that is needed to get started on making a print room.*

OPPOSITE *A collection of classical figure prints look particularly striking against a strong coloured background. A coat of clear varnish protects the prints.*

Hanging the prints

There are several different ways to go about pasting and hanging, and as you proceed you will probably develop your own method. But the following is effective as a starting point. First, cut out all the prints and borders. However much border is cut, you are almost certain to need more; it is difficult to judge the amount until you are arranging it, and then you will be surprised by how quickly it gets used up.

Cut the borders with mitred corners: this can be done quite simply by folding the border over at an angle of 45 degrees and cutting along the fold, but to be certain of a good finish only mitre one side. Leave the other side straight and paste the mitred corner over it. How to mitre borders is explained in more detail on page 179.

Start by placing the biggest prints on the wall. Begin with the most important position, which will usually be over the fireplace or on the wall opposite the window. At this stage attach the prints to the wall with Blu-Tack so you can alter the placing easily. Achieving an attractive result is usually a question of trial and error, of arranging and rearranging the prints until they are successfully grouped. Think in groups of pictures, and try to avoid equal spacing between groups, as this creates a less pleasing effect. Balance, however, is vital. The easiest way to achieve a balanced design is to use pairs of prints, starting with one large central picture flanked by smaller ones above and below or side by side. Add the borders next, making sure that the frames do not overpower the pictures. Finally add the decorative details – for example, ribbons and chains to link the prints, bows to hang them, and a selection of trophies and ornaments to embellish the whole group. Again, time spent creating the composition is the most vital aspect of making a harmonious design, so continue to experiment until you are completely satisfied; then leave the arrangement for a day or two to be sure it works. Make

tiny dots on the wall with a pencil to mark placements when you remove the prints for the final pasting up of the print-room design.

First dampen the prints with a wet sponge on the wrong side and then apply ready-mixed wallpaper paste or a starch paste. If the paste seems too thick and lumpy, add a little water. Make sure the paste covers the piece completely, especially the edges of intricate designs. Let the print absorb the paste briefly and then remove any excess with a soft cloth. Place the print on the wall, smoothing out any air bubbles with a soft cloth or paperhanging brush. Then hang the borders around the prints and finally paste up the bows, chains, ribbons and swags. Do this before the paste has dried on the borders so the chains and ribbons can be tucked underneath the edges. If you have covered a wall in a busy area such as a hall or stairway, you can protect the design by varnishing the entire wall when the prints have dried. Use an acrylic varnish, as oil will discolour the paper.

Using framed pictures

When a collection of prints is too precious to be pasted directly to the wall, or you wish to make a decoration which you can take with you when you move, you can still create a print room effect with mounted and framed prints, hanging them in groups and decorating with swags and bows. A specialist framing company will make frames in a variety of shapes, so you can design the arrangements using square pictures, octagons, ovals and rectangles. The grouping of the pictures is important, but they will obviously be too heavy for you to tack temporarily to the wall. A practical solution is to plan the arrangement of both pictures and decorative paper elements on the floor. Measure the distances between the pictures. Hang the most important picture and then arrange the others around it according to the measurements you have taken. Once you are sure that the picture hooks are in the correct place, you can temporarily remove the pictures while you paste the paper decorations on the wall.

Designing with modern prints

A print room using modern prints in colour can be designed in much the same way as the traditional room, but you may prefer to use simpler borders than those made available on published print room sheets. Wallpaper borders are often suitable and can be chosen to complement the colours of the prints. It is best to select fairly simple designs. Some borders showing architectural mouldings work well, but they may need to be cut down so as not to overpower the prints. You can create variations by using Italian marbled paper, cut into strips, to make borders. Some subjects look best with a plain border, rather like a mount, and this is very easy to hang. Cut a plain piece of coloured paper slightly larger than the print, and paste the print on top of the paper, allowing an equal border all around. Then print and border are pasted together on the wall.

With coloured prints it is better to use coloured bows and ribbons to provide the additional decoration. Some manufacturers produce wallpaper patterns or borders from which suitable bows can be cut, or you can use wall decorations which are already cut out.

OPPOSITE *A contemporary interpretation of the print room theme by artist Andrea Maflin stimulates the diners in this London club restaurant.*

o desiderio ·

pigliai questa fatica :

F stampa, le quali tanto se auuicinano alle scrit pigliai questa fatica. E perche impossi te a mano, quanto capena il mio ingegno, E se de mia mano porger tanti essempi, ch

e fantazzate E non trahezate E f per ebc io restit variacione de lettera la qual im = ferire

technique library

Equipment and materials

Having the right tools for the job is essential for successful paperhanging and makes all the difference between a professional finish and less-than-perfect results. The correct equipment is not expensive and is readily available from any good do-it-yourself or hardware store. If you are using old or borrowed tools, they must be in good condition to produce successful results and, above all, clean.

PASTING BRUSH/ROLLER

You can use a wide paintbrush for pasting, but a special pasting brush, with more flexible bristles, makes it easier to spread the paste evenly.

In the case of certain highly absorbent papers it is preferable to apply the paste directly to the wall, rather than to the paper. If this is necessary, it will be stated on the label. For this you will need a paint roller and tray for the paste.

PAPERHANGER'S BRUSH

This is a wide brush with thick, soft bristles used for smoothing the paper once it is on the wall. The handle is shaped so that it can be held comfortably and used with light pressure to ease the paper into corners and angles of the wall without tearing it.

Professionals use hanging brushes measuring 30–33cm (12–13in) in width, but these can be awkward for a beginner to handle; a brush about 23cm (9in) wide is about right.

SEAM ROLLER

A felt or rubber roller is useful for smoothing down the joins between lengths of paper. A wooden or plastic roller can be used for borders but will make a hard line if used on a wallpaper join.

WALLPAPER SHEARS AND SCISSORS

A good pair of wallpaper shears will make the paperhanger's job much easier. They are large, with blades about 15cm (6in) in length, for making long cuts. The points are specially shaped to crease the paper as it meets an angle, giving a line to cut along.

Do not be tempted to use dressmaking or kitchen scissors as you may get jagged cuts. You will, however, need a small pair of ordinary sharp-pointed scissors for snipping and trimming.

TRIMMING KNIFE

In some tight corners, a knife is more useful than scissors. Together with a steel rule, it can also be used to cut long, straight lines. A craft knife with replaceable blades is ideal. Make sure that the blade is very sharp for precision cutting.

STEEL RULE

Professionals use a long metal metre rule or yardstick and a trimming knife for cutting straight lines down the length of the wallpaper. An ordinary short ruler is much harder to manage and usually results in wavy lines. You will also need a short metal ruler and a retractable steel tape measure.

PLUMB LINE AND CHALK

A plumb line consists of a string with a weight attached. It is used to mark vertical lines on the wall so that the paper can be positioned to hang absolutely straight. You can either buy a plumb line or make one with some non-stretch string and a small, flat, heavy object. You will also need some chalk or charcoal to rub into the string in order to mark the vertical on the wall.

SPIRIT LEVEL

A spirit level can be placed either horizontally or vertically alongside a border or pencilled guideline to check that it is straight. If it is, the air bubble appears exactly in the centre of the glass tube in the spirit level.

PASTING TABLE

Any reasonably long table is suitable for pasting, as long as its surface will not be damaged by paste or water. There are cheap, lightweight tables built for the purpose. They can be folded away when not in use. They are also narrower than conventional tables, making pasting easier.

STEPLADDER

A stable stepladder is vital for paperhanging; balancing on a chair or a stool is not safe and rather difficult. An aluminium stepladder is lightweight and easy to move around, and one with a platform as the top step is useful for holding equipment.

If you are papering a ceiling, you will need an extra stepladder and a wooden plank or a multipurpose ladder.

ADHESIVE

Different kinds of wallpaper require different kinds of paste. Buy the paper first, and follow the manufacturer's recommendations regarding paste; this is vital for a successful result.

SIZE

A coating of size (generally a dilution of the wallpaper paste) is necessary to prevent the adhesive from soaking into the walls and producing dry spots under the wallpaper. It also facilitates repositioning the paper on the wall. Size can be applied with an ordinary paintbrush or with a pasting brush.

The label on the paper will specify which kind of size to use.

BUCKETS, SPONGE, CLOTHS

You will need two buckets, one for the paste and another larger one for water. You will also need a soft cellulose sponge to wipe off any paste that gets onto the wallpaper surface. This is more suitable than a cloth and can be quickly rinsed in clean water if it becomes sticky.

You will also need plenty of soft, clean cloths, for more general cleaning up, and some old sheets or dust sheets to protect the floor and furniture.

OTHER TOOLS AND MATERIALS

Various other tools and materials may be required for preparing the wall surface. These might include fine sandpaper, a filling compound for cracks and holes, a filler knife, a scraper and wire brush for removing old wallpaper, a steam stripper, primer and sealer. These items are described in greater detail in the section on 'Preparing walls for papering' on page 166.

Estimating quantities

There are several variables to consider when calculating the amount of wallpaper you will need: the dimensions of the room, the width and length per roll of the paper you have chosen (both of which vary according to the manufacturer and the country of origin), and the length of the pattern repeat. Your interior design or decorating store will certainly advise on quantities but will need accurate measurements of the room in order to provide a correct estimate.

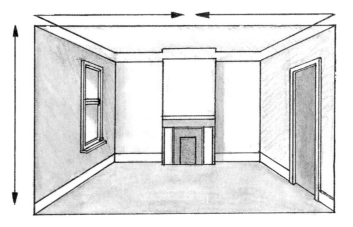

MEASURING THE ROOM

1 First measure around the entire room, including doors and windows, alcoves and mantelpieces.

Then measure the height of the room from the ceiling or base of the cornice down to the skirting (base) board. Measure between picture rail and/or dado rail if you are confining the paper to this area.

2 If the paper is plain or has a pattern that does not require matching, add 10cm (4in) to the height measurement for trimming – 5cm (2in) at both top and bottom. This gives the length of a drop, or full length of paper.

If the paper has a pattern repeat, each length will have to be hung at the same level, but the entire length of the repeat (as well as the 10cm/4in) must be added to each drop, so that you can position the pattern correctly.

Some wallpapers with very large repeats should be hung using alternate rolls, which will minimize wastage. In the sample book you will find precise instructions on allowing for the repeat.

CALCULATING THE AMOUNT TO BUY

1 Once you have chosen the paper, divide the total distance around the room (obtained in step 1 of 'Measuring the room') by the width of the paper. This gives the number of drops you will need.

2 Now divide the length of the roll by the length of a drop (again, see step 1, 'Measuring the room') to get the number of drops that can be cut from each roll.

It is safest to include fireplaces, windows and doors in these calculations, even though this will entail some wastage. However, if you are intending to use an expensive paper, ask the supplier to adjust the number of drops to allow for these openings.

3 Finally, divide the total number of drops required by the number of drops per roll; this is the number of rolls you need to buy. It is a good idea to add a roll to this total to allow for mistakes in cutting or for spoiling a length when hanging. Buy all the rolls at the outset, making sure that they are from the same printing batch; the number is printed on the label. Colours vary, if only slightly, from one batch to another, and variations will show up on the wall. If you have underestimated and need more rolls, quote the batch number when re-ordering and check the rolls on delivery to make sure that they are from the same batch.

Preparing walls for papering

The quality of the finished result depends on the condition of the wall surface beneath the paper. So do not be tempted to neglect the preparation in your eagerness to get on with the creative part of the job.

The amount of preparation required varies according to the paper chosen. With a textured paper or a lively print, slight irregularities will probably not be visible, whereas with a subtle stripe or a plain paper they may be glaringly evident. If in doubt, err on the side of caution.

Before starting work on preparing the walls for papering, remove as much furniture as you can from the room to allow you freedom of movement. Move any remaining heavy furniture to the centre of the room and cover it with dust sheets (drop cloths) for protection while work is in progress.

Whether you are papering over new dry wall, newly plastered walls or previously papered walls, the walls must be sound, smooth and dry.

NOTE Walls to be papered may be first sized, usually with a weak solution of wallpaper paste and water, to keep the wall from absorbing paste too quickly. A number of combination primer-sealers are available specifically designed to prepare walls to be papered over. Your retail wallpaper centre can advise you as to which one is right for your job. No matter what kind of wall you are papering over, you may need to apply sizing or a wallcovering primer as the last step before hanging the paper or paper lining.

REMOVING OLD WALLPAPER

It is advisable to remove old wallpaper before applying new. The original paper may be on the verge of coming loose, and a new layer would hasten the process. New paper should never be applied over metallic, flocked, washable or vinyl papers.

For removing old paper the basic equipment is a scraper (a knife resembling a putty knife but with a stiff blade), a wire brush, a bucket of warm water and a sponge.

1 Score the surface of the paper with the wire brush. (Some scrapers have a serrated edge which can be used for this.) This helps the water penetrate the surface and soften the paste.

2 Soak the wall thoroughly with warm water: a few drops of vinegar or liquid detergent added to the water will help the soaking process.

3 Use the scraper to remove the paper, taking care not to dig in to the plaster **(A)**. Resoak the walls as necessary.

If the wallpaper resists ordinary soaking, it can be loosened with a proprietary chemical stripper. Choose one intended for wallpaper and follow the manufacturer's instructions when using it.

In very stubborn cases, or if you want to do the job speedily, use a steam wallpaper stripper. You can rent one inexpensively from a do-it-yourself shop. Simply apply the steam pad directly to the wall with one hand while scraping the previously softened adjacent area with the other **(B)**. The steamer will speed up the process; however, there is some risk of loosening the plaster, and you may prefer to get professional help with this job.

REPAIRING HOLES AND CRACKS

For this you will need a resin-based filling compound, available in both ready-mixed and powder form, and a putty filler knife with a wide, flexible, squared-off blade to enable you fill holes and cracks.

1 First remove any loose plaster. If you are filling a crack, undercut it first to provide a secure grip for the filling **(C)**. Using a scraper, cut into the crack diagonally to form a V shape, with the widest part of the V inside. Brush out all loose plaster.

A

B

C

D

2 Apply the filler with the putty knife, pressing the blade flat over the hole **(D)**. Make sure that no air is trapped under the filler.

3 When the hole or crack is filled, scrape the knife across the top, to remove the excess and make the surface as smooth as possible.

If a hole is large, fill it in stages, applying the filler in layers about 3mm/⅛in thick and allowing each to dry before adding the next one.

4 When the filler has dried, rub the surface down with fine sandpaper.

PAPERING OVER DRY OR PLASTERED WALLS

1 Make sure the surface is dry, clean and free of dust. (Newly plastered walls need at least 6 weeks to dry out fully before they can be papered.) In most cases, you will simply need to wipe away all flecks of dust with a clean cloth and make sure that the walls are dry.

2 Apply a wallcovering primer or size. For a new dry wall, it may be necessary to use at least two coats of primer. For cement walls, apply a masonry sealer, then a wallcovering primer. Allow the sealer to dry thoroughly.

PAPERING OVER PAINT

1 Make sure any repair compound is completely dry. For freshly painted walls, allow at least 30 days to dry.

2 Wash the walls with water and a mild detergent solution. Allow to dry and then sand with fine sandpaper. Wipe away dust particles.

3 Apply a wallcovering primer or size. If you are papering over a dark paint colour and the wallpaper that you have chosen is thin, you may need to use a white-pigmented wallcovering primer. Leave it to dry thoroughly.

Lining walls

Some people think that a lining paper is unnecessary, but if you want to get a completely smooth and professional finish it is essential. Because it is neutral in colour, lining paper is especially useful when applying a light-coloured wallpaper over a wall that has previously been painted a dark colour. It also gives you the chance to practise hanging paper and to solve the problems of a particular room before attempting the final papering. Lining paper comes in several weights; a medium-weight paper is suitable for most purposes. With it you should use the size and adhesive recommended for the top paper.

E

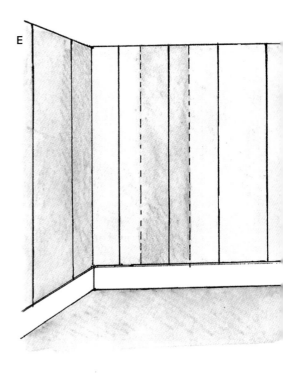

HANGING LINING PAPER

Professional decorators hang lining paper horizontally (called cross-lining) which prevents any possibility of the seams of the two layers coinciding. However, this is a tricky manoeuvre, and the inexperienced paperhanger should hang the lining paper vertically, following the instructions given below for hanging the top paper. (If you do wish to cross-line, follow the instructions for hanging horizontally on page 181.)

Begin at the point chosen for the first drop (see page 168), but hang the first drop of lining paper slightly to the left or the right of this position **(E)**. In this way, the joins will be staggered. At corners, trim the paper and butt the edges together (rather than overlapping them, as when hanging top paper at corners). Allow the lining paper to dry before hanging the top paper.

Papering walls

If you are intending to paper both walls and ceiling, tackle the ceiling first. Instructions for papering ceilings are given on pages 176-177.

Before beginning to hang the wallpaper you should plan positioning carefully. The first length should be positioned at the focal point of the room. This might be above the fireplace, the wall between two windows or the centre of the most important wall. Start in the middle of this wall and work out to either side.

If the paper is patterned, decide on the place where it will meet; since the pattern is unlikely to match precisely it should be an inconspicuous place such as an inner corner near a door.

Plain wallpapers are much easier to hang than patterned ones because there is no design to match. A small, regular pattern will present few problems, but a large pattern repeat requires care in cutting the first drop to make sure that the design looks balanced on the wall. Hold the first length against the wall before cutting to determine the ideal position and also to make sure that it is the right way up. (Even professionals have been known to hang paper upside down!) Hang a complete motif at the top, rather than cutting it through the middle.

A

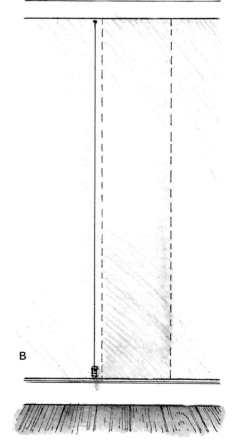

B

CUTTING THE LENGTHS

Cut a number of drops – enough for one wall, or perhaps for the whole room – and then paste and hang a few of these at a time.

1 Measure and cut the first drop, allowing 10cm (4in) extra for trimming 5cm (2in) at both top and bottom.

2 Cut the following drops, holding each one next to the previous one as shown and adjusting it to match the pattern before cutting **(A)**. (Papers with little or no pattern can simply be placed on top of the first drop and cut to the same length.)

If the paper has a large repeat, cut the lengths from two different rolls, alternately, following the manufacturer's instructions, to minimize wastage.

Cut the lengths on the pasting table, first having made sure that there is no paste on it. As a precaution you might cover the table with a length of lining paper and move this along or replace it if you get paste on it.

If you are matching a large pattern, you may find it more comfortable to cut on the floor, rather than on the narrow pasting table.

FINDING THE TRUE VERTICAL

Before you hang the first drop, you must mark a true vertical line on the wall. Do not rely on windows or doors being straight or even parallel to each other; if you do, the result is likely to be a vertical slant all the way around the room. Use a plumb line to mark the wall where one edge of the paper will be placed.

1 Find the centre point for the first strip, then measure off to one side half the width of the paper. Mark this point at the top of the wall.

2 Measure off a length of string the distance from the ceiling or cornice to the skirting (base) board. Rub chalk into the string (use charcoal, if the surface is light). Tie one end to the weight, and fasten the other with a nail to the mark at the top of the wall **(B)**.

3 When the plumb line is hanging still, hold the weight firmly against the skirting (base) board and flick the string so it rebounds against the wall. This will accurately mark a vertical line.

PASTING THE PAPER

1 Lay the paper face down on the pasting table, with one edge overlapping the table slightly and the lower end hanging off the end of the table. Secure it at the upper end with the shears or another heavy object to prevent it from rolling up.

2 Starting at the upper end, apply a line of paste down the centre of the paper, then paste out to the overlapping edge, covering the paper evenly with criss-crossing diagonal strokes **(C)**. Apply the paste generously; difficulties in hanging paper, such as air bubbles, often arise from having used too little paste. Take care to avoid lumps.

3 Slide the paper so that the unpasted edge slightly overlaps the table, and paste to the edge in the same way. Make sure that the edges are well covered with wallpaper paste.

4 Fold the pasted end over so that it lies somewhat past the middle of the drop, then slide the unpasted end up onto the table. Paste this end in the same way, and fold it to meet the other end. The shorter fold at the lower end makes it easy to distinguish top from bottom **(D)**. Be careful not to crease the paper.

5 Lay the folded paper on the floor, and allow the paste to soak into it for a few minutes so that it becomes pliable; follow the manufacturer's recommendations for the time. This is important because too little soaking may result in bubbles. Too much, and the paste will dry before you have got it on the wall. When the paper is ready for hanging, lift it as shown **(E)**.

READY-PASTED PAPERS

Ready-pasted papers come with a tray, or trough, for wetting. Cut the paper into lengths as for an unpasted paper. Partially fill the tray with water, and place it next to the wall where the strip is to be hung; roll up the paper loosely, with the top edge on the outside, and immerse it in the tray for the length of time specified by the manufacturer. Then gently unroll the paper **(F)** and apply it to the wall as described on page 170.

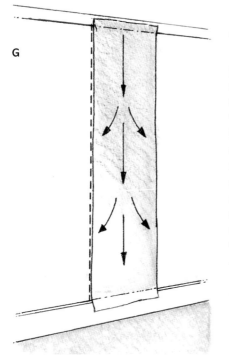

G

TO HANG THE PAPER

1 Unfold the top end of the paper and place it against the wall, holding the upper edge approximately 5cm (2in) above the top of the wall and lining the vertical edge up to the chalked vertical line. Make sure that the paper falls straight down the chalk line, adjusting it if necessary. If the positioning is incorrect, gently lift the paper from the bottom and readjust it. Use the hanging brush to smooth the paper very lightly down the middle and out towards the sides, working downwards **(G)**, and removing any large air bubbles by lifting and repositioning it. (When the paper is still damp small bubbles may be noticeable but these will disappear as it dries.)

2 To finish the top edge, trim with a craft knife or push the tips of the shears against the ceiling line to crease the paper slightly **(H)**. Peel the paper gently back or use wallpaper shears to cut evenly along the fold line **(I)**. Then brush the paper back into place. Repeat the process at the lower edge. The edges can be pressed down gently with a felt roller, but avoid too much pressure, which will cause a line or indentation. Wipe off excess paste from the ceiling, skirting (base) board or paper.

3 To hang the second length, cut and paste as described above. Line it up against the first strip with the edges butted together, not overlapping. Continue until you reach a corner, where a different technique (see below) is required.

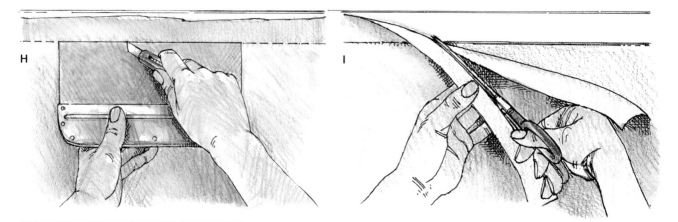

H

I

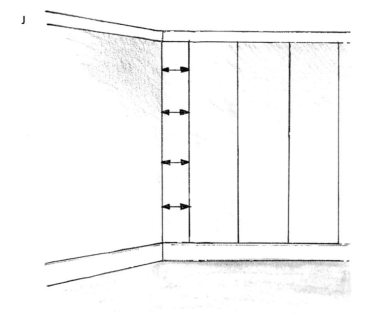

J

PAPERING ROUND CORNERS

Do not attempt to fold a large area of paper around a corner, because it will not hang straight. Paper the corner in two stages, as described below. The technique is essentially the same for inner and outer corners.

1 When the last full width near a corner has been pasted, measure the remaining distance. Measure at several points down the wall **(J)**, because the distance may vary. Take the greatest distance and add 5mm (¼in) to it. This is the required width of the drop.

2 Mark this width on the paper and carefully cut, using the steel rule as a guide for a perfectly straight line.

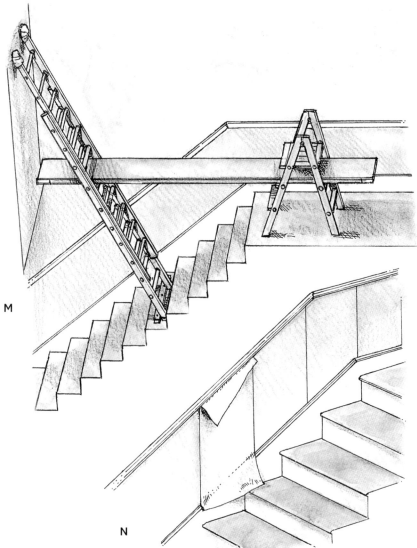

M

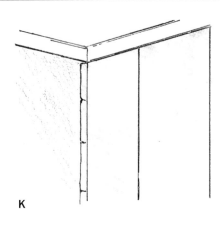

N

HANGING PAPER ALONG STAIRS

Papering a stairwell, or even a single long flight of stairs, is really a job for a professional. It requires at least two ladders, plus one or more platforms, all rigged together securely. The ladders must be fixed to the floor and/or stair treads (with the carpet first removed) by means of battens nailed securely in place **(M)**. Needless to say, a good head for heights is also essential.

It is relatively easy, however, to paper alongside a short flight of steps, where the ladder can simply be placed at the top of the steps and then at the bottom. In this case, the only special technique is trimming the lower edge at an angle.

Cut the paper to measure the distance to the lowest point of the slope, adding the usual allowances (see page 168) for trimming and pattern matching. Then, after positioning the drop, press the blades of the scissors into the groove at the skirting (baseboard), pull the paper away, and trim along the crease. Press the trimmed paper into place.

Essentially the same technique is used at the upper edge if you are hanging a dado along stairs. In this case the paper is creased along the lower edge of the dado rail **(N)**.

3 Paste and hang the partial width in the usual way, taking the extra 5mm (¼in) around the corner. On an inner corner, brush it firmly into the corner using the tips of the bristles. If the wall is uneven, make tiny snips in the turned edge so that it will lie smoothly **(K)**.
4 Measure from the corner a distance equal to the width of the paper left over when you cut the previous drop, plus 5mm (¼in), and mark a vertical at this point with a plumb line.
5 Cut a drop of wallpaper to this width. The cut edge will overlap the previously pasted drop by about 5mm (¼in). The outer edge is pasted to align with the new vertical **(L)**.

K

If you are hanging a vinyl paper you will need to use a latex adhesive where the edges overlap. Roll the edge firmly with a seam roller to ensure a secure join.

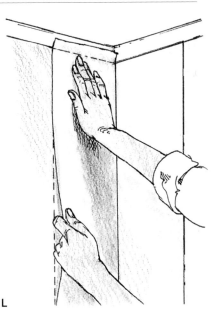

L

DOORS AND WINDOWS

Papering around doors and windows requires different techniques, depending on the structure and moulding surrounding the window.

NON-RECESSED DOORS AND WINDOWS

1 Hang the first overlapping length untrimmed **(A)**.
2 Cut around the frame, leaving an overlap of about 5cm (2in). Press the paper against the frame to mark the corner. Cut diagonally into the corner **(B)**.

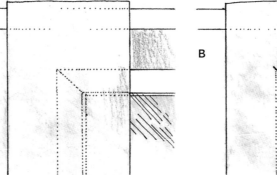

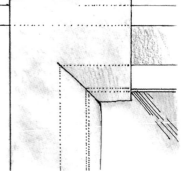

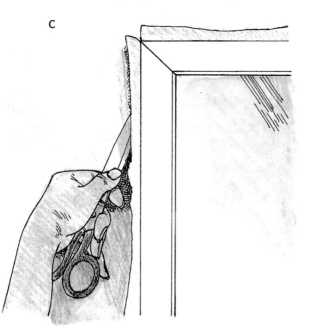

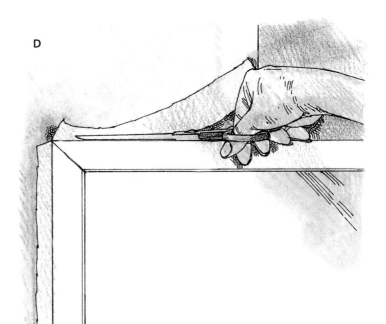

3 Press the paper into place, creasing it firmly with the shears **(C)**, and trim as usual, with the knife or scissors, taking care not to tear the paper at the corner **(D)**.
4 At the lower edge of a window frame the procedure is basically the same as at the top, although a projecting sill requires a slightly different technique at the corners. Let the paper hang over the windowsill, then cut horizontally through the paper. Snip the edges **(E)**, taking care not to cut too deeply, push the paper into the angle **(F)** and trim.
5 Hang short lengths above and below the frame in the usual way, then hang the next full drop as described in steps 1–3 above.

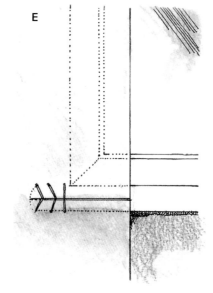

SHALLOW RECESSED WINDOWS

If the window is set in from the wall by only a small amount – 3cm (1in) or so – you can just turn the paper round the edge of the wall. First trim it to measure slightly more than the required amount, then press it into the edge of the window frame, crease and trim to fit.

If the reveal is deeper – up to 20cm (8in) – you can take the side edge round the corner as shown below.

1 When you hang the full drop along the side edge of the reveal, do not stick it down firmly. Cut along the upper edge of the recess and the sill **(G)**.

2 Cut a piece to fit into the top of the reveal at the corner **(H)**. This should measure the depth of the reveal **(a–b)** plus 3cm (1in) for turning up at the front; in width it should be the distance from the corner of the reveal to the edge of the wallpaper above **(c–d)** (so that the

seams will be aligned) plus about 3cm (1in) to turn down at the corner.

3 Gently peeling back the full drop, paste this piece into the upper corner of the reveal **(I)**, taking care to align its edge with that of the upper piece; press the other edge into the corner.

4 Paste the free vertical edge of the main strip to the side of the reveal. Short drops above the window should be cut long enough to cover the top of the reveal **(J)**.

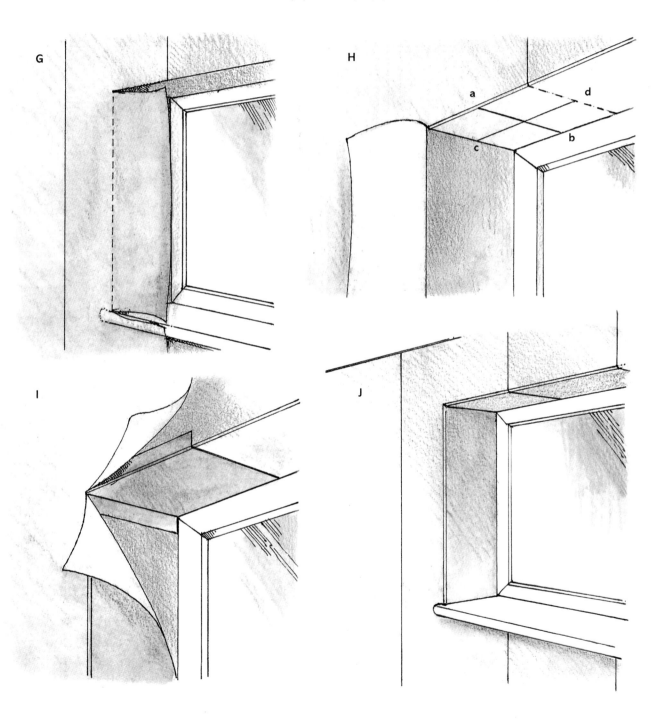

DEEPLY RECESSED OR BAY WINDOWS

If you wish to paper the ceiling as well as the sides of a deeply recessed window with a paper that has a noticeable pattern, it is possible to get a perfect match by following the hanging sequence suggested in the sketch **(K)**. If your paper is plain or has a tiny repeating motif, the hanging sequence is not so crucial.

If the wallpaper happens to end with a complete drop at the edge of the recess, it is quite simple to paper the ceiling and walls in the sequence shown, so that the joins fall in the same position.

However, this recommended order – while explaining the principle behind achieving a successful match – is only a guide. The individual window and the position in which the seams fall on the main wall may dictate a slightly different order of hanging.

ARCHWAYS

Paper the wall first, then start papering the inside of the arch.

1 After papering the wall, trim the excess to about 3cm (1in) or so. Snip into the excess to ease it around the curve and turn the edges to the underside of the arch. Cut off any tiny overlapping bits to make the surface as smooth as possible **(L)**. Repeat this process on the other side of the arch, if necessary.

2 Cut the strip for the inner arch to the exact width of the arch. If the paper has a noticeable vertical repeat, cut two strips, each slightly longer than the height, to be joined at the centre.

3 Fold the strip concertina-like and paste it in place **(M)**. If you are using two strips, overlap their upper edges at the centre, cut through both strips with a knife, remove the offcuts and butt the trimmed ends together.

For an arched recess the process is similar, but before hanging the strip(s) on the arch, paper the inner wall area. If the arch has a steep slope, like a Gothic arch, the paper may be trimmed slightly to shape to make it easier to fit the apex of the arch. But beware of cutting away too much. Snip the paper edges and paste them to the inside of the arch. Make sure to align the seams and the wallpaper pattern repeat.

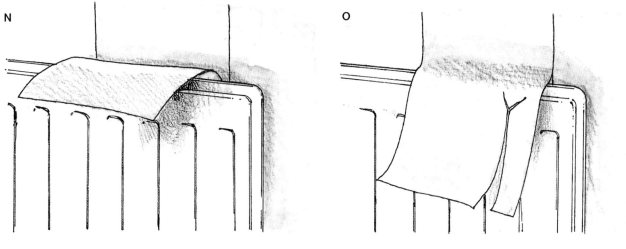

RADIATORS

1 Cut and paste a full drop of paper, but only smooth the top half onto the wall. Press the lower end down onto the top brackets that secure the radiator to the wall **(N)**.

2 Pull the paper out, then cut upwards from the lower edge to the creases marking the bracket positions, making a V shape at the top **(O)**.

3 Smooth the lower end down behind the radiator, using a cloth wrapped around a long stick.

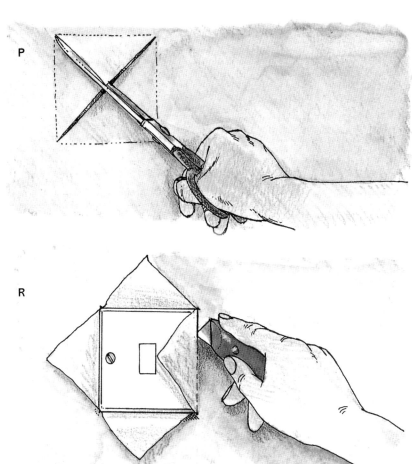

ELECTRIC SOCKETS AND LIGHT SWITCHES

First turn off the electricity at the fusebox.

1 Hang the paper and smooth it gently over the switch or socket plate to reveal the outline.

2 Cut diagonally from the centre of the shape almost to each corner **(P)** and peel the paper back.

3 If possible, loosen the screws holding the switch plate, trim the paper edges to within about 1cm (½in) of the plate edge **(Q)** and slip them under the plate. Tighten the screws. *(Important: Do not use this method with foil or metallic papers, which conduct electricity.)* Alternatively, simply crease the edges of the flaps closely around the switch or socket plate and trim them with a knife **(R)**.

REHANGING PICTURES

If you want to rehang pictures or bookshelf brackets in the same position as before you started decorating, mark their positions with matchsticks. Insert the matchsticks in the holes, then break them off close to the wall surface. Press the paper gently over the matchsticks so that it is pierced neatly.

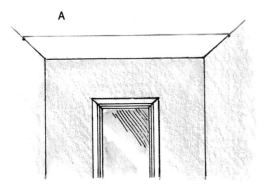

A

Papering ceilings

Although there are fewer obstructions to deal with, papering a ceiling is considerably more difficult than papering a wall – simply in terms of the physical effort – and is best not attempted by the novice. If you do need to paper a ceiling, enlist a helper, and take special care to set up a secure working platform.

You will need either two stepladders and a plank or decorators' trestles, rented from do-it-yourself shops. Prepare the ceiling as described for walls, pages 166–167.

The ceiling of the room should be papered before the walls, and the paper should be hung parallel to a wall containing a window, beginning at that wall and working away from it.

1 Measure inwards along the ceiling from the starting wall, and mark off a distance about 3cm (1in) less than the width of the roll of paper at both sides of the ceiling. Rub chalk or charcoal into a piece of string and fasten the string to the ceiling at both points **(A)**. Snap the string to mark a line on the ceiling.

2 Remove the string and measure along the line. Cut the first strip to this measurement plus about 10cm (4in). Cut the remaining strips, adding extra for matching the pattern, if any, and adjusting the length for any wider parts of the room.

3 Paste each length as described on page 169, but fold it concertina-style to make it easy to handle **(B)**.

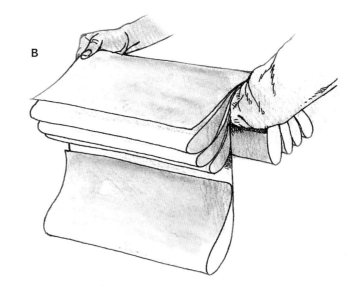

B

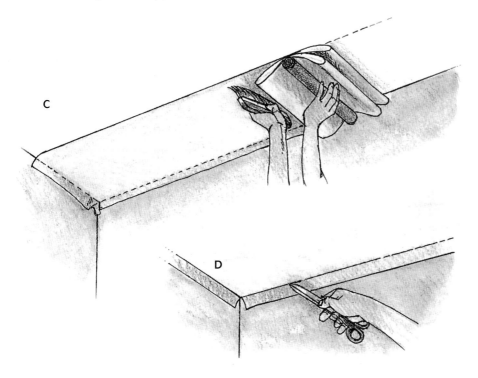

C

D

4 Place the platform directly under the chalked line. Unfold the top end of the paper and smooth it in place along the chalked line, supporting the folds with a cardboard tube. Gently press the excess into the angle with the wall, using the paperhanger's brush. Move along the platform, unfolding the paper and smoothing it in place. Make sure you keep the edge aligned with the chalked line **(C)**.

5 Cut into the corners to enable the excess paper to lie flat. Press the edges firmly into the angle, using shears **(D)**. Pull the ends away from the wall, and trim them to about 1cm (½in). Brush the paper back into place. If the walls are not to be papered, trim the edges precisely.

6 Without moving the platform, hang the next length of paper, butting its edge to the previously pasted edge. When hanging subsequent lengths, move the platform directly under the edge of the previously pasted length.

CEILING ROSES

First turn off the electricity at the fusebox and remove the shade and bulb.

1 Paper up to the rose and press the paper against the flex outlet to mark the central point. Cut a cross at this point large enough to slip the lampholder and flex through.

2 Enlarge the cross, cutting it in triangular flaps so that the rose cover will slip through it. Unscrew the rose cover, then carefully trim back the flaps of paper with the scissors **(E)**. Lastly, screw the rose cover back in place.

To paper around the corner of an alcove or recess, cut the paper diagonally **(F, G)**, and trim away the excess.

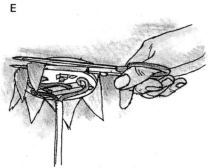

E

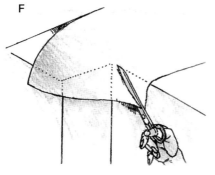

F

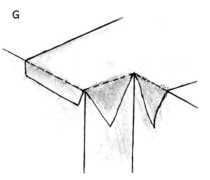

G

MITRED STRIPED CEILING

A mitred striped ceiling is less difficult to paper than it may appear. Since the ceiling is divided into four sections, the drops of paper are shorter than normal and therefore relatively easy to handle.

1 Using string rubbed with chalk or charcoal (see page 168), mark diagonal lines on the ceiling **(H)**.

2 Having thus located the mid-point of the ceiling, measure the length of each wall and mark the halfway point. Mark chalked lines joining these points to the centre point. The central stripe of the wallpaper must run down these lines.

3 If the centre stripe of the paper corresponds with the centre of the roll, as is normally the case, measure off half the width of the wallpaper to one side and mark another chalk line straight across the ceiling to indicate the edge of the first strip of paper.

Mark a similar guideline at right angles to this one **(I)**.

If your stripe design is not centred on the roll you will have to adjust these guidelines accordingly.

4 Cut the first drop to measure from one wall to the centre point, adding the usual allowance for trimming.

5 Paste the drop to the ceiling, aligning one edge with the straight chalked line, and overlapping the centre point slightly. Smooth it lightly in position, then pull back the edges along the diagonal lines, crease

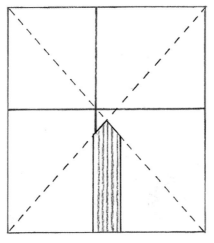

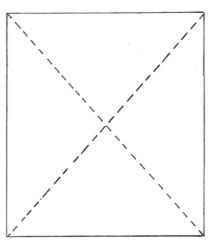

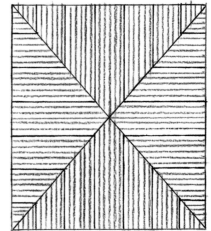

and trim **(J)**. Absolute accuracy is not essential, as the edges will be covered with a border. Trim the edge at the wall.

6 Apply the adjacent, shorter drops in the same way to fill this first section of the ceiling (K).

7 Repeat steps 3–5 in the remaining sections of wall.

Borders, dados and friezes

Wherever you are hanging a border, it must be straight. Unless you have an existing straight line to work to – a dado or picture rail, for example – you will have to draw a guideline. If you wish to hang a border next to an uneven or sloping ceiling, the irregularity will be less noticeable if you take it from the lowest point of the ceiling, hang it straight and paint the exposed area above the border the same colour as the ceiling.

MEASURING QUANTITIES

For a simple border along the top of the wall, measure round the entire room. Double this if you are bordering the skirting (base) board, too, but deduct the width of the door(s).

Measure around doors and windows if they are to be bordered, adding a little extra for mitring corners. Add the height of the room if you intend to border the walls at the sides. Remember to take the border up both walls at the corner. Allow a little extra for errors.

MARKING GUIDELINES

These are essential if you are to achieve a professional-looking finish.

BORDERS AT PICTURE RAIL LEVEL

1 Measure down from the ceiling and mark the wall very lightly with a pencil at several points. Using a straight edge as a guide, join these points to indicate the edge of the border.
2 Check with a spirit level that the line is exactly horizontal.

BORDERS AT DADO LEVEL

1 Measure up from the skirting board at intervals; join the line and check with a spirit level.
2 To hang the border on a diagonal up the stairs, mark a vertical at the top and bottom of the slope, using a plumb line (see page 168). Measure up from the skirting (basboard) at both points and mark the height of the border.
3 Mark the height of the border at intervals between these points and join the marks using a straight edge. Alternatively, fasten a chalk line between the top and lower points and flick it against the wall to mark a guideline.

OUTLINING DOORS AND WINDOWS

Hang the border up to the edge of the frame. If it appears to be crooked, ease it – while the paste is still damp – closer or further away from the frame as necessary.

APPLYING BORDERS

Use a strong ready-mixed tub paste or a special border adhesive.

1 Cut a length of border, making it as long as possible.
2 Cover the pasting table with a sheet of lining paper, which can be changed as necessary. Apply the paste generously using a pasting brush and taking care to paste thoroughly to the edges to prevent peeling. This is especially important with borders that have curved or angled edges. As you paste, fold the border concertina-style **(A)**. This makes it easier to handle.
3 Ideally, hang the border from right to left if you are right-handed; from left to right if you are left-handed. Smooth it lightly in place with a cloth as you go along. Then, when you are confident that it is correct, go over it more firmly, taking special care to press down the edges with a seam roller. Wipe excess paste away carefully with a damp sponge **(B)**.
4 At a join, overlap the paper slightly unless this spoils the wallpaper pattern match **(C)**. If this is the case, butt up to the joins instead, pasting them firmly together so they do not open to leave an obvious gap when dry.

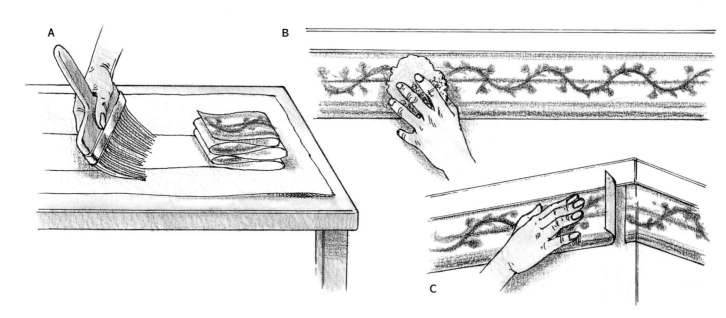

A

B

C

MITRING RIGHT-ANGLED CORNERS

Use one of the following methods to mitre the corners of the border as you proceed. Instructions for matching large patterns at corners are given on pages 182–183.

METHOD 1

1 Paste the vertical border to the wall, leaving the end square and taking it to the outer edge of the border position.

2 Cut the horizontal border slightly longer than required, and paste it to the wall, almost up to the vertical strip. Fold it back so that it makes a 45° angle, matching the pattern on the vertical border **(D)**. Crease it sharply along this fold, and cut along the crease.

3 Paste it over the vertical strip **(E)**. The advantage of this method is that even if the cut is slightly inaccurate, or if the border should shrink a little, there is never a gap.

METHOD 2

1 Cut both borders slightly longer than necessary and paste to the wall, lapping one corner over the other. Cut diagonally through both strips **(F)**, using a metal straight edge and a knife.

2 Paste the trimmed edges in place **(G)**. This is a simpler method and results in a smooth butt join. The same method is used if you are joining borders at different angles, or if you need to mitre a succession of difficult angles – for example, around a fireplace with a stepped outline.

A slight curve can be followed by snipping the border at regular intervals almost all the way across it and then overlapping the edges **(H)**. The pattern will be distorted slightly, so bear this in mind when choosing the border.

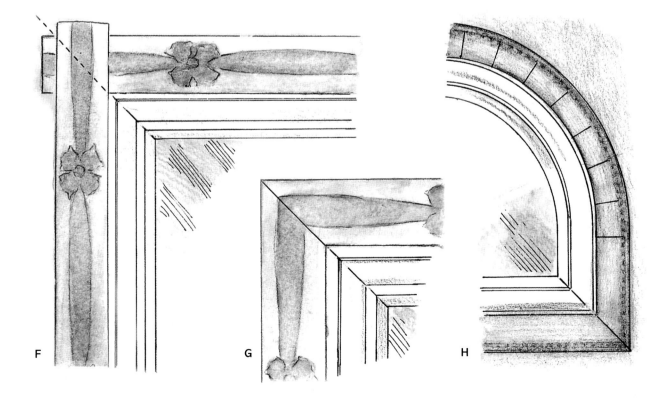

MEASURING UP AND HANGING BORDERS

Borders supplied in separate pieces such as the Gothick arch border shown on page 148 can be made to fit any wall length exactly, with the swags always finishing perfectly in the corners.

1 Measure the length of each wall. Then measure the length of one swag. Divide the wall measurement by this figure to give the number of swags needed. If there is a small amount over, use it up by leaving gaps between the pieces **(A)** to be covered by rosettes. If the swags take up slightly less space than the wall length, overlap the pieces **(B)** and cover the joins. With some designs the joins are not covered, but the amount of overlap is varied to ensure an exact fit **(C, D)**.

2 It is easiest to lay the swags out on the floor to check the layout, leaving equal gaps between them or overlapping them as necessary.

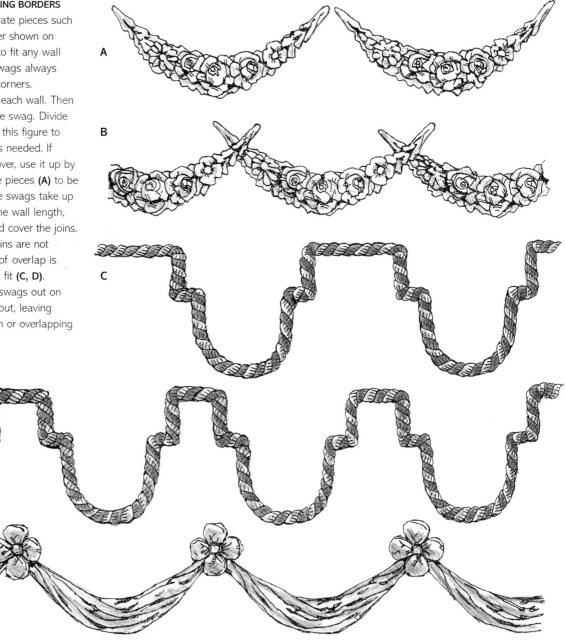

A

B

C

D

E

Alternatively, you can measure the wall, marking the position of each decorative element exactly.

3 Repeat this process for the other walls.

4 Paste the swags (as instructed on page 178). If appropriate, cover the gaps or overlaps with rosettes, bows or knots **(E)**.

5 At the corners, fix the rosettes, bows or knots so they are centred on the wall angle to give a continuous effect **(F)**.

F

PHOTOCOPIED BORDERS

1 Once you have chosen your border design, enlarge or reduce it if necessary to the required depth **(G)**. Make several copies of this size, and paste them to a sheet of A3 paper (11 x 14 in). By using larger paper you keep the number of joins to a minimum, and fitting several side by side reduces the cost.

2 Photocopy this page onto good-quality paper – white, if you wish to colour the design later, or tinted paper if you want a two-tone effect **(H)**. Spray with artists' fixative so that the ink does not smudge. Commercial photocopiers will usually have a range of suitable papers, or will use paper that you provide. It is important to choose one that is reasonably thick; otherwise it may crumple and crease when hung.

3 Cut out the border pieces, using a metal straight edge and knife if the edges are straight, or scissors if they are curved, and paste them to the wall. Join the edges together carefully **(I)** to give a continuous design.

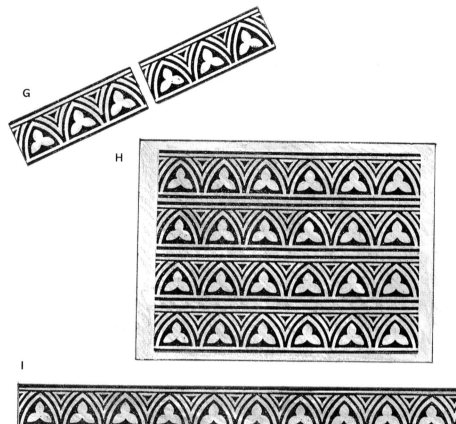

G

H

I

HANGING DADOS AND FRIEZES

A dado is hung just like a full-length drop of paper, except that the upper edge is trimmed to fit snugly under the dado rail. Instructions on hanging dados up staircases are given on page 171. Friezes can be treated as extra-wide borders (see page 178).

To hang a width of wallpaper horizontally to make a dado or frieze, measure and cut the paper to the length of the wall. A length of paper will normally turn around a mantelpiece or shallow window without falling out of alignment, but do not attempt to take very long lengths of paper round corners. If you need a guideline, follow the method for marking one suggested on page 178.

Paste the paper in the normal way (see page 169), allowing the paste to soak into it until it is pliable. Then fold the paper loosely into a manageable concertina. Starting in a corner, paste down one end and begin to unfold the rest of the strip, smoothing the paper to the wall as you go **(J)**. When hanging paper horizontally in a dado, you may need to use more than one width of the paper. Start under the dado rail and work downwards. Cut the second piece about 2.5cm (1in) deeper than needed before pasting it. Smooth into position, trimming any excess above the skirting (base) board **(K)**.

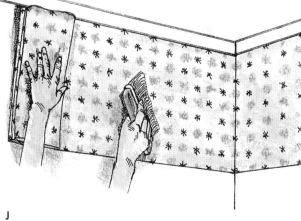

J

K

Panels

It may be helpful to begin by drawing a plan of the walls on graph paper including the position of doors and windows. Start by deciding on the position of the most important panel. This might be in the middle of the main wall or over the fireplace. Then decide on the arrangement of panels on either side. The spacing and arrangement of the panels should be adjusted to suit the room. As a general rule, the spacing around the panels should be equal, but you may allow a slightly deeper space between the base of the panel and the skirting (base) board.

If you are making outline panels with borders, draw them to scale and experiment with different proportions. Panels filled with a contrasting paper can be arranged like outline panels. Alternatively, you can make each panel the exact width of your wallpaper and run borders around the edge to form the frame, adjusting the space between panels to fill the wall. It may also be possible to use half the width or a width-and-a-half of the wallpaper to create a complete motif within the panel.

Special effects, such as the arrangement shown on page 124, should be planned carefully on the graph-paper plan. If the wallpaper has little or no pattern, cut small pieces of it and move them around on your plan until you are pleased with the arrangement.

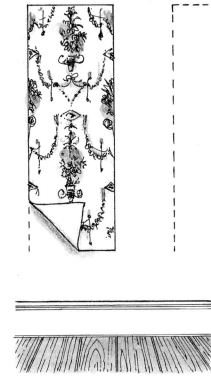

B

A

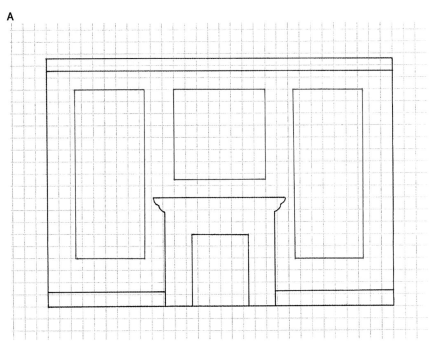

HANGING PANELS

1 If you are working out the panel size and position on graph paper, calculate the measurements of each panel using your chosen scale: for example, each square = 10cm (6in). Include the measurements between the panels and the space between panels and floor/ceiling **(A)**.

2 Mark the positions of the panels on the wall, following the plan. Start with the top horizontal line, using a straight edge and spirit level (see page 164) for accuracy. Then mark the verticals with a plumb line (see page 164). If you are marking the position of decorative filler paper, you only need mark one vertical. Lastly, mark the bottom horizontal.

3 If you are using a decorative filler inside the borders, cut this to size first. Use a set square and straight edge to ensure 90° angles on the corners. Paste the panel to the wall, according to the horizontal lines and butting the plumb line **(B)**.

4 When the panels are hung, add the border strips using one of the methods suggested on page 179 to mitre the corners of the paper.

HANGING BORDERS WITH LARGE REPEATS

If you are making a panel with a border that has a large repeat, it will not be possible to get all the corners to match evenly. Make sure that the top corners are perfect as these are the most noticeable. Before cutting the border strips to length, select the joining point on one strip of border and mark and trim the diagonal edge with a transparent set square **(C)**.

Position the edge over the adjacent strip at the joining point **(D)** and lightly mark the angle. Then paste the border to the wall, sliding it into position and adjusting it until the motifs match perfectly.

If you are placing prints within the space, these are stuck down after the border, but their positions should first be carefully planned on the squared paper and then marked on the wall.

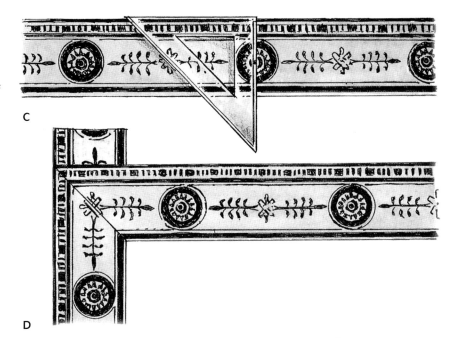

C

D

Cut-out decorations

If an arrangement is fairly complicated, carefully measure it out on the wall surface, and position it temporarily with Blu-Tack. This gives you a chance to check the final position of the design before pasting it in place. Mark the positions of each paper decoration lightly with pencil or use the temporarily stuck pieces as a guide for positioning, as you paste each motif in place.

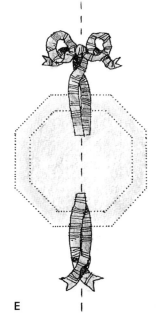

E

DECORATIVE FOCAL POINTS

To make a decorative arrangement like the one over the fireplace on page 149, experiment first to find the best positions for the separate elements. Hang the pieces with Blu-Tack and mark their position lightly in pencil. Paste each piece in place, starting with the larger ones. Cover joins with bows, rosettes or knots.

If a rope or ribbon is intended to look as if it supports a wall-hung object, such as a picture or plate, mark the position of that object first. A single piece can be cut to appear above and below the plate or picture **(E)**; it need not continue behind it.

CEILING DECORATIONS

Exact mathematical precision is not essential, as you will rarely look straight up at the ceiling, but a formal arrangement of cut-out decorations does depend on symmetry. Mark the centre point of the

ceiling, as described on page 177, and use this as a position guide.

PASTING

Use a good-quality wallpaper paste or border adhesive. Cover each piece generously and evenly and allow to soak for at least five minutes before applying it to the wall.

Intricately shaped pieces are very fragile when wet and should be handled with great care to avoid tearing. Once applied to the wall, however, they can be repositioned with a gentle sliding movement. Smooth them down with a clean cloth, roll the edges firmly with a seam roller and wipe off any excess paste using a damp cloth.

PASTING PRINTS DIRECTLY TO THE WALL

The best adhesive is a starch paste. A border adhesive may be suitable, but if it

is too wet the paper may buckle; a dry spray-mount will give a flat finish but the corners may begin to peel after a time. Experiment with different pastes to find the one that works best with the thickness of your paper. Photocopies on a thin paper may need to be mounted on a light cardboard before pasting, so that the paper does not crumple and crease when pasted to the wall surface.

bibliography

Beard, Geoffrey
Craftsmen and Interior Decoration in England 1660–1820
John Bartholomew & Sons, London 1981

Belanger Grafton, Carol
Silhouettes
Dover Publications, London 1979

Bredif, Josette
Classic Printed Textiles from France 1760–1843:
Toiles de Jouy
Thames & Hudson, London 1989

Cornforth, John
The Inspiration of the Past
Viking, London 1985

Entwisle, E.A.
The Book of Wallpaper
Kingsmead, London 1954

Fowler, John and Cornforth, John
English Decoration in the Eighteenth Century
Barrie & Jenkins, London 1974

Greysmith, Brenda
Wallpaper
Studio Vista, London 1976

Hamilton, Jean
An Introduction to Wallpaper
Victoria and Albert Museum, London 1983

Hapgood, Marilyn
Wallpaper and the Artist
Abbeville Press, New York 1992

Hoskins, Lesley (editor)
The Papered Wall
Harry N. Abrahams 1994

Jacqué, Bernard
Le Papier Peint: Décor d'Illusion
Florilege Gyss Editeurs, Rixheim 1989

Jones, Chester
Colefax & Fowler: The Best in English Interior Decoration
Barrie & Jenkins, London 1989

Jones, Owen
The Grammar of Ornament
Studio Editions, London 1986 (1856)

Lynn, Catherine
Wallpaper in America
A Barra Foundation/Cooper-Hewitt Museum Book
W.W. Norton & Company, New York 1980

McCelland, Nancy
Historic Wallpapers
J.B. Lippincott, Philadelphia 1924

Nouvel-Kammerer, Odile
Papiers Peints Français 1800–1850
Office du Livre, Paris 1981
Papiers Peints Panoramiques
Musée des Arts Décoratifs/Flammarion, Paris 1990

Nylander, Richard C.
Wallpapers for Historic Buildings
The Preservation Press, Washington, DC 1983

Oman, Charles C. and Hamilton, Jean
Wallpapers
Sotheby Publications, London 1982

Teynac, Françoise, Nolot, Pierre & Vivien, Jean-Denis
Wallpaper, A History
Thames & Hudson, London 1982

Thornton, Peter
Authentic Decor: The Domestic Interior 1620–1920
Weidenfeld & Nicolson, London 1984

Turner, Mark and Hoskins, Lesley
Silver Studio of Design
Webb & Bower, London 1988

The Victoria & Albert Colour Books
Ornate Wallpapers
Webb & Bower, London 1985

suppliers

Wallpapers for photography were supplied by the following.

2 Ornamenta Ltd
5 Sanderson & Sons Ltd
6 Ornamenta Ltd
7 De Gournay Ltd
8 Ornamenta Ltd
9 Paper Moon
11 Deborah Bowness
14 Zuber & Cie
17 De Gournay Ltd
21 Brunschwig & Fils
22 Zoffany Ltd
26 Cole & Son Ltd
27 Cole & Son Ltd
42 Maya Romanoff
43 Zuber & Cie
44 Muriel Short Designs
46 Brian Yates Interiors Ltd
48 Zoffany Ltd
49 Mulberry Company
53 Brunschwig & Fils
53 John Oliver
   at Paper Library
56 Ornamenta Ltd
57 Brunschwig & Fils
   and Alexander Beauchamp
59 Nobilis-Fontan Ltd
60 Designers Guild
61 Baer & Ingram
62 Brian Yates Interiors Ltd
63 Designers Guild
65 Osborne & Little Plc
66 Ornamenta Ltd
67 Osborne & Little Plc
68 Ornamenta Ltd
69 Ornamenta Ltd
70 Osborne & Little Plc
72 Nono Designs Ltd
73 Ottilie Stevenson Ltd
74 Brian Yates Interiors Ltd
75 Neisha Crosland
   at Paper Library
78 Ornamenta Ltd

79 Ornamenta Ltd
80 Graham & Brown
81 Osborne & Little Plc
82 Nono Designs Ltd
83 Ornamenta Ltd
84 Osborne & Little Plc
85 Brian Yates Interiors Ltd
86 Ornamenta Ltd
87 Graham & Brown
88 Ornamenta Ltd
89 Maya Romanoff
90 Vymura
91 Brian Yates Interiors Ltd
92 Nobilis-Fontan Ltd
94 Maya Romanoff
95 Anaglypta
96 Brian Yates Interiors Ltd
97 **Top to bottom**
   Gijs Bakker Design
   Brian Yates Interiors Ltd
98 Maya Romanoff
99 Osborne & Little Plc
100 Maya Romanoff
101 Nobilis-Fontan Ltd
102 Nina Campbell
   at Osborne & Little Plc
103 Nina Campbell
   at Osborne & Little Plc
104 Sanderson & Sons Ltd
105 Cath Kidston
106 Paper Library
107 Paper Library
108 Paper Library
109 Colourlink
110 Colourlink
111 Jocelyn Warner
112 Tracy Kendall
113 Sharon Elphick
114 Vymura
117 Anna French Ltd
118 Cole & Son Ltd
118 Cole & Son Ltd
121 Ornamenta Ltd
121 Muriel Short Designs
   and Cole & Son
124 Nobilis-Fontan Ltd

125 Anna French Ltd
126 Nobilis-Fontan Ltd
129 De Gournay Ltd
130 De Gournay Ltd
132 Farrow & Ball
133 Nono Designs Ltd
134 Designers Guild
135 Nono Designs Ltd
138 Ornamenta Ltd
139 **Top to bottom**
   Scalamandré
   Osborne & Little
   Zoffany
   Schumacher & Co
   Osborne & Little
   Cole & Son
   Laura Ashley
   Massacco
   Brunschwig & Fils
141 Alexander Beauchamp
146 Ornamenta Ltd
   Cowtan & Tout
   Sanderson & Sons Ltd
147 Ornamenta Ltd
148 Ornamenta Ltd
149 Ornamenta Ltd
150 Nicola Wingate-Saul
   and Ornamenta Ltd
157 Lewis & Wood
158 Ornamenta Ltd
160 Andrea Maflin Partnership
162 Hill & Knowles

directory

• For information on wallpaper, go to the Wallcoverings Association home page at **www.wallcoverings.org**

• To locate stores in the U.S. and Canada that carry the Waverly line of wallpapers (and many other brands), go to **www.waverly.com** or call 800 423 5881

• **www.wallpaperstore.com** and **www.decoratetoday.com** are excellent on-line wallpaper centers

Note In the following listing, those sources that sell directly to the retail consumer and/or can provide a list of stores that carry their products are marked with an asterisk (★).

Anaglypta
Crown Wallpaper
2485 West 2nd Avenue
Suite 18
Denver, CO 80223
Tel: 800 422 2099

Anna French Ltd
Classic Revivals Inc
Suite 534, 5th Floor
1 Design Center Place
Boston, MA 02210
Tel: 617 574 9030

Anya Larkin
8th Floor
39 West 28th Street
New York, NY 10001
Tel: 212 532 3263

Baer & Ingram
Davan Industries
404 Pleasantview Court
Kopiague, NY 11726
Tel: 516 944 6498

Brian Yates
Available through
Sanderson & Sons Ltd

Brunschwig & Fils
for a list of showrooms, go to
www.brunschwig.com

Chesapeake Wallcoverings ★
401-H Prince George's Blvd.
Upper Marlboro, MD 20774
Tel: 800 275 2037
www.cheswall.com

Christopher Hyland, Inc.
D & D Building
979 Third Avenue
New York, NY 10022
Tel: 212 688 6121

Colefax & Fowler Group Plc
Available through Cowtan & Tout

Cowtan & Tout
979 Third Avenue
New York, NY 10022
Tel: 212 753 4488

Crown Wallpaper
Crown Corporation
Denver, CO 80202
Tel: 800 422 2099

De Gournay Ltd
Sloan Miyasato
2 Henry Adams Street
Suite 207
San Francisco, CA 94103
Tel: 415 431 1465

Decorating Den Interiors ★
19100 Montgomery Village Avenue
Montgomery Village, MD 20886
Tel: 800 332 3367
www.decoratingden.com

Note Decorating Den is a U.S./Canada network of decorator franchises. Call or visit their Web site for locations.

The Design Archives
Available through Lee Jofa

Designers Guild
Available through
Osborne & Little Plc

Donghia
485 Broadway
New York, NY 10013
Tel: 212 925 2777

Duron Paints & Wallcoverings ★
Fort Lauderdale, Atlanta, Chicago,
Richmond, King of Prussia (PA)
Beltsville (MD)
Tel: 800 723 8766
www.duron.com

G.P. & J. Baker Ltd
Available through Lee Jofa

Graham & Brown Inc
2031 U.S. Route 130
Monmouth Junction, NJ 08852
Tel: 732 940 0887

Home Depot ★
Various locations; consult your
Yellow Pages

House of Wallcoverings Inc ★
4141 NE 2nd Avenue
Miami, FL 33137
Tel: 305 576 0048

Imperial Wallcoverings ★
23645 Mercantile Road
Beechwood, OH 44122
Tel: 800 539 5399
www.imp-wall.com

Janovic Plaza *
Various locations in New York City.
Consult your Yellow Pages.

Laura Ashley Inc *
For a Laura Ashley home furnishings
store locator, go to
www.laura-ashleyusa.com

Lee Jofa
For a list of Lee Jofa showrooms, go to
www.leejofa.com

The Maya Romanoff Corporation
1730 West Greenleaf
Chicago, IL 60626
Tel: 773 465 6909

Massacco
53 Leonard Street
New York, NY 10013
Tel: 212 925 8667

Mulberry Company
Available through Lee Jofa

Muriel Short Designs
Available through Scalamandré

Nessen
Suite B260
1855 Griffin Road
Dania Beach, FL 33004
Tel: 954 925 0606

Nobilis
57a Industrial Road
Berkeley Heights, NJ 07922
Tel: 908 464 1177

Ornamenta Ltd
Stark
979 Third Avenue
New York, NY 10022
Tel: 212 752 9000

Osborne & Little Plc
90 Commerce Road
Stamford, CT 06902
Tel: 203 359 1500

Ottilie Stevenson Ltd
Watkins and Fonthill
D& D Building
979 Third Avenue
New York, NY 10022
Tel: 212 755 6700

Nina Campbell
Available through Osborne & Little

Paper Library
Watkins and Fonthill
D& D Building
979 Third Avenue
New York, NY 10022
Tel: 212 755 6700

Scalamandré
942 Third Avenue
New York, NY 10022
Tel: 800 932 4361
www.scalamandre.com

Schumacher & Co
939 Third Avenue
New York, NY 10022
Tel: 212 415 3900
www.fschumacher.com

Seabrook Wallcoverings Inc *
1315 Farmville Road
Memphis, TN 38122
Tel: 800 238 9152
www.seabrookwallcoverings.com

Seamans Discount Wallpaper *
166 Spring Street
Dexter, ME 04930
Tel: 207 924 5600
www.seamanswallpaper.com

Studio E Inc
450 W. 31st Street, 7th Floor
New York, NY 10001
Tel: 212 244 2800

Turnell & Gigon
Available through Schumacher & Co

Warner Fabrics plc
Whittaker & Woods
51000 Highlands Parkway
Symrna, GA 30082
Tel: 770 435 9720

Warner Wallcoverings *
The Warner Company
108 South Desplaines Street
Chicago, IL 60661
Tel: 800 685 8822
www.thewarnerco.com

Watts of Westminster
Christopher Norman Inc.,
979 Third Avenue
New York, NY 10022
Tel: 212 644 4100

Zimmer & Rohde
D & D Building
979 Third Avenue
Suite 1616
New York, NY 10022
Tel: 212 758 5357

Zoffany Ltd
Whittaker & Woods
51000 Highlands Parkway
Symrna, GA 30082
Tel: 800 395 8760

Zuber & Cie
D & D Building
979 Third Avenue
New York, NY 10022
Tel: 212 486 9226

index

acknowledgments

Author's Acknowledgments

The production of this book was an enjoyable project to work on, because it reconnected me with many of my friends and contacts. It also introduced me to the talented duo of Walton and Pringle, with whom it has been a delight to work. It was thanks to Carey Smith, senior editor at Frances Lincoln, that the idea to publish the book was formed, and Caroline Thomas, the picture researcher responded to every suggestion and tracked down even the most esoteric sources. I am very grateful for their talent and professionalism.

At the beginning, in the research stages, several museum curators and librarians generously gave the benefit of their time and experience and pointed me in the right direction for further study. In France Bernard Jacqué at the Musée du Papier Peint in Rixheim and Véronique de Bruignac at the Musée des Arts Décoratifs in Paris kindly showed me part of their comprehensive wallpaper collections. Most helpful also were Crosby Forbes at the Peabody Museum of Salem, Massachusetts, Elizabeth Padjen, Richard Nylander at the S.P.N.E.A. in Boston, Massachusetts, Heather Wood at the Royal Pavilion in Brighton, the staff of the wallpaper collection at the Victoria and Albert Museum in London, the curators of many National Trust properties and the owners of historic houses containing beautiful antique wallpapers.

The time taken up by such a project has had an impact on my own wallpaper company, Ornamenta, and I would particularly like to thank Louise Latham and Sally Crawford for their constant help and good humour as the project progressed. My wallpaper printers are skilled and careful exponents of their craft and have taught me almost everything I know about making beautiful wallpaper, so I would like to recognize the generosity of Allan and Alexander Bruce, Michael Balcock and James Gillespie, Miles Thacker and Dale Gessey in sharing their very considerable knowledge. My thanks also go to colleagues in other wallpaper companies who, over the course of several years, have helped me with advice and information, Anthony Evans, Denis Hall, Karen Beauchamp and Fiona Flint.

Photographic credits

2: Ornamenta Ltd/photo: John Gott; 5: Sanderson; 6: Ornamenta Ltd/photo: John Gott; 7: De Gournay; 8: Ornamenta Ltd; 9: PaperMoon; 10: Colourlink Creative Imaging/artist: Simon Henwood; 11: Deb Bowness/photo: Karen Hatch; 12-13: 'Cow' paper by Andy Warhol © The Andy Warhol Foundation for the Visual Arts, Inc., ARS, NY and DACS, London 2000; 14: Zuber; 15: Montage devised by Christian Von Heusinger, 20" x 12", The Metropolitan Museum of Art, Rogers Fund, 1922. (22.97.4,5); 16: Victoria & Albert Museum, London (by courtesy of the Board of Trustees); 17: De Gournay: 18: © Frances Lincoln/ Tim Imrie (Courtesy of The Directors of Coutts & Co); 19: Arcaid/ Lucinda Lambton; 20: Arcaid/ Robert Benson; 21cr: Brunschwig & Fils; 21 cl: Zoffany; 22: Zoffany; 23: World of Interiors/ James Mortimer; 24: John Hall; 25: The Interior Archive/ Fritz von der Schulenburg; 26: Cole & Son (Wallpapers) Ltd; 28: Bracken Books, London; 29: Arcaid/Richard Bryant; 30: Grategus, 1901 by CFA Voysey, The Whitworth Art Gallery, The University of Manchester; 33: Alen MacWeeney; 34: V&A Picture Library; 37: V&A Picture Library; 38: Bridget Riley; 40-41: Anaglypta; 42: Maya Romanoff Corporation; 43: Zuber; 44: Muriel Short; 45: Arcaid/ Mark Fiennes; 46: Brian Yates; 47: © Frances Lincoln/ Tim Imrie; 48: Zoffany; 49: Mulberry; 50: Boys Syndication/ Michael Boys; 51: © Frances Lincoln/ Tim Imrie; 52: John Hall; 53: Brunschwig & Fils; 53: © Frances Lincoln/ Tim Imrie; 54: Derry Moore; 56: Ornamenta Ltd; 57: © Frances Lincoln/ Tim Imrie; 59: Colin Walton; 60: Designers Guild (for stockists please call Designers Guild on 020 7243 7300); 61: Baer & Ingram; 62: Brian Yates; 63: Designers Guild (for stockists please call Designers Guild on 020 7243 7300); 65: Osborne & Little; 66: Ornamenta Ltd; 67: Osborne & Little; 68: Ornamenta Ltd; 69: Ornamenta Ltd; 70: Osborne & Little; 71: Peter Woloszynski; 72: Nono; 73: Ottilie Stevenson; 74: Brian Yates; 75: Neisha Crosland; 76-77: Benetton; 78: Ornamenta Ltd; 79: Ornamenta Ltd; 80: Graham & Brown; 81: Osborne & Little; 82: Nono; 83: Ornamenta Ltd; 84: Osborne & Little; 85: Brian Yates; 86: Ornamenta Ltd; 87: Graham & Brown; 88: Ornamenta Ltd; 89: Maya Romanoff Corporation; 90: Vymura; 91: Brian Yates; 92: Colin Walton; 93: The Interior Archive/ Simon Upton; 94: Maya Romanoff Corporation; 95: Anaglypta; 96: Brian Yates; 97b: Brian Yates; 97cr: Droog; 98: Maya Romanoff Corporation; 99: Osborne & Little; 100: Maya Romanoff Corporation; 101: Colin Walton; 102: Osborne & Little/ Nina Campbell; 103: Osborne & Little/ Nina Campbell; 104: Sanderson; 105: Cath Kidston; 106: Paper Library; 107: Paper Library; 108: Colourlink Creative Imaging/ artist: Judy Phillips; 109: Paper Library; 110: Colourlink Creative Imaging/ artist: Ella Doran; 111: Jocelyn Warner; 112: Tracy Kendall/ photo Colin Walton; 113: Sharon Elphick/ photo: Colin Walton; 114-115: Vymura; 116: Collection du Musée des Arts Décoratifs, Paris/ photo M.A.D./ L. Sully-Jaulmes; 117: Anna French; 118: Cole & Son; 120r: © Frances Lincoln/ Tim Imrie: 120l: Nobilis-Fontan Ltd; 121: Ornamenta Ltd; 122: © Frances Lincoln/ Tim Imrie; 123: Nobilis-Fontan Ltd; 124: Nobilis-Fontan Ltd; 125: Anna French; 126: © Frances Lincoln/ Tim Imrie; 127: Historisches Museum, Basel/ Maurice Babey; 128: Lars Hallen; 129: De Gournay; 130: De Gournay; 131: Collection du Musée des Arts Décoratifs, Paris/ photo M.A.D./ L. Sully-Jaulmes; 132: Farrow & Ball; 133: Nono; 134: Designers Guild (for stockists please call Designers Guild on 020 7243 7300); 135: Nono; 136: Peo Eriksson; 137: John Hall; 138: Ornamenta Ltd; 139: © Frances Lincoln/ Tim Imrie; 140: © Frances Lincoln/ Tim Imrie; 141: © Frances Lincoln/ Tim Imrie; 143: Victoria & Albert Museum, London (by courtesy of the Board of Trustees); 144: World Press Network Ltd/ IPC Magazines; 145: World Press Network Ltd/ IPC Magazines; 146: © Frances Lincoln/ Tim Imrie; 147: © Frances Lincoln/ Tim Imrie; 148: © Frances Lincoln/ Tim Imrie; 149: Ornamenta Ltd; 150: © Frances Lincoln/ Tim Imrie; 151: Castledown Foundation Ltd; 152l: © Frances Lincoln (Designer John Sutcliffe) / Tim Imrie; 152r: Ianthe Ruthven; 153: Derry Moore; 154: © Frances Lincoln (Designer John Sutcliffe) / Tim Imrie; 156: Derry Moore; 157: Lewis & Wood; 158: Ornamenta Ltd; 159: © Frances Lincoln/ Ianthe Ruthven (Nicola Wingate-Saul print rooms made by Denise Czyrka); 160: Andrea Maflin/ Designer: Annie Waite; 162-163: Hill & Knowles